JAMES BRENIG

First Coins

Foundations of Wealth

First published by Governor's Yard Publishing 2025

Copyright © 2025 by James Brenig

All rights reserved. No part of this publication may be reproduced, stored or transmitted in any form or by any means, electronic, mechanical, photocopying, recording, scanning, or otherwise without written permission from the publisher. It is illegal to copy this book, post it to a website, or distribute it by any other means without permission.

This novel is entirely a work of fiction. The names, characters and incidents portrayed in it are the work of the author's imagination. Any resemblance to actual persons, living or dead, events or localities is entirely coincidental.

James Brenig asserts the moral right to be identified as the author of this work.

James Brenig has no responsibility for the persistence or accuracy of URLs for external or third-party Internet Websites referred to in this publication and does not guarantee that any content on such Websites is, or will remain, accurate or appropriate.

Designations used by companies to distinguish their products are often claimed as trademarks. All brand names and product names used in this book and on its cover are trade names, service marks, trademarks and registered trademarks of their respective owners. The publishers and the book are not associated with any product or vendor mentioned in this book. None of the companies referenced within the book have endorsed the book.

First edition

ISBN (paperback): 9798275885040

Contents

Authors note	v
Introduction	1
1 The Boy Who Was Always Broke	3
2 The Secret of the First Coin	12
3 Coins That Grow While You Sleep	28
4 The Deal That Looked Too Perfect	48
5 A Home of Your Own	66
6 Future You	81
7 Levelling Up Your Skills	96
8 Escaping the Debt Trap	110
9 What Does "Rich" Even Mean?	126
10 The Bag That Wasn't Theirs	151
11 The Test of a Hundred Coins	169
12 Full Circle	190
13 Real World Examples	206

Dedicated to my son Eli, whose curiosity and character inspired these lessons on life, value, and purpose.

May your journey always be guided by wisdom, kindness, and the courage to think differently.

Authors note

When I first read The Richest Man in Babylon, I was struck by how simple, honest, and powerful the lessons were. Yet, I also realised that if I had read it as a teenager, I probably would not have understood half of it, not because the ideas were hard, but because the world it described was so different from ours and the language was so difficult.

Today, we live in a world of instant everything: instant messages, instant entertainment, and instant spending. We are surrounded by opportunities, but also by distractions. And the most important lessons about money, saving, investing, giving, and patience, can easily get lost in the noise.

That is why I created First Coins. It is not about becoming rich overnight or chasing success that looks good online. It is about understanding the timeless rules that have guided every generation toward independence, stability, and purpose.

The stories in this book are inspired by the wisdom of Babylon, retold for a new generation. I have rewritten them in modern language, added real world examples, and adapted the narrative so it is easier to follow as you journey with Nadan and his friends through their challenges and choices.

Whether you are earning your first pocket money, saving for something big, or just starting to think about your future, this book is your guide to building habits that last a lifetime.

Start small.
  Stay consistent.
  Think long-term.

The first coin is always the hardest to save, but it is also the most important.

Introduction

Money is confusing.

You are expected to know how to use it, but almost nobody really explains it. You probably hear things like:
"Just save more."
"Do not waste your money."
"Invest early."

Okay... how?
What does that actually look like with your life, your bank account (or lack of one), your friends, your parents, your future?

Almost a hundred years ago, a writer collected simple money stories and set them in an ancient city called Babylon. Adults still read that book, The Richest Man in Babylon, because the rules inside it are simple and powerful: money is not the goal, it is a tool.

This book takes those ideas and retells them as a story for you. No "thy gold." No fake complicated finance talk. Just a group of teenagers in ancient Babylon figuring out how to stop being broke and start taking money seriously.

Think of it as your first financial map, not a lecture but a compass. You will learn how to:

- Keep part of everything you earn
- Avoid traps that drain your money
- Make your savings work for you
- Build a reputation of trust and value
- Use money as a tool for freedom, not pressure
- Avoid dumb mistakes that can cost you years

You do not need to wait until adulthood to understand wealth. You only need curiosity, consistency, and a few good habits, starting with your first coin.

Ready?

Let's go to Babylon.

1

The Boy Who Was Always Broke

Babylon was hot, noisy, and full of people who seemed to be in a hurry.

Merchants shouted prices over each other. Donkeys pulled heavy carts through narrow streets. The smell of bread, sweat, and spices mixed in the air. Somewhere in that mess walked a boy named **Nadan**, counting the last three copper coins in his hand.

"Three coins," he muttered. "And payday is five days away. Again."

He slipped the coins into his belt pouch and sighed. He worked as an assistant to a scribe, copying tablets and running messages. It wasn't glamorous, but it did pay. The problem wasn't what he *earned*.

The problem was that his money always disappeared.

He knew the pattern by heart:

1. **Payday** – feeling rich, promising himself he'll save this time.
2. **Next day** – buying sweet cakes with friends to celebrate.
3. **Two days later** – new sandals because the old ones were "embarrassing."
4. **End of the week** – empty pouch, small regret, big shrug.
5. **Repeat.**

Today, he walked through the market and pretended not to look at things he couldn't afford.

A shiny flute.
   A carved wooden horse.
   A small, beautiful clay lion that would look perfect on his shelf.

He stopped, staring at the lion.

"How much?" he asked the seller.

"Two coins," the man said. "A bargain."

Nadan had three coins. He could buy the lion and still have one coin left. One coin was better than nothing, right?

His hand moved towards his pouch, then he heard his name.

"Nadan! Hey!"

He turned to see **Bela**, his best friend, weaving through the crowd, waving one arm and nearly dropping a round loaf of bread with the other.

Bela was always eating.

"You're late," Nadan said.

"You're always broke," Bela replied with a grin. "Come on, the others are waiting. We're meeting under the palm tree."

"The Empty Pockets Club meets again," Nadan said dryly.

They had started the "club" as a joke. It was just a few friends who all had the same problem: **money came in, money went out, none stayed**.

The palm tree stood near the edge of the city, where the walls looked out over the fields. In its shade sat **Daria**, sharp-eyed and serious, and **Karim**, who was trying to juggle three stones and failing.

The ground around them was dusty. Their problems felt bigger.

"You're late," Daria said to them both.

"We were busy being broke," Bela said, tearing his bread loaf in half and tossing a piece to Nadan.

Nadan caught it. "Thanks," he said automatically, then

frowned. "I should pay you back for this."

"With what?" Daria asked. "Those two coins you're hiding in your pouch?"

Nadan glared. "Three coins," he said quietly. The clay lion flashed in his mind. "Probably."

Daria leaned back against the tree trunk. "Exactly. That's why we're here."

Karim dropped all three stones and groaned. "I'm tired of it. Every time I get a little money, it vanishes. My father says, 'You must learn to control your spending, son.' Then he walks away without explaining anything."

"Same," Bela said. "My uncle told me, 'Make your money work for you.' How? Does it grow legs and walk to the market?" He kicked at the dirt. "No one actually shows us how."

The four of them fell quiet. A group of older men walked past, laughing about something. One of them wore elegant, perfectly cut yet simple robes, he had no gold jewellery or flashy chains, yet the air around him seemed to part for his step. Nadan recognised him.

"That's **Arkad**," he said. "The richest man in Babylon."

They all watched Arkad and his companions. Even from a distance, he looked different: relaxed, not rushing, not worried.

Karim spoke first. "Imagine if we had his money. We'd never be in this mess."

Daria shook her head. "Lots of people win and then lose money. I've seen it. The real question is: **how did he get it, and keep it?**"

Bela chewed thoughtfully. "My father says Arkad used to be poor. A scribe like you, Nadan."

Nadan blinked. "No way."

"That's what he told me," Bela said. "He said Arkad learned special rules about money."

Nadan stared after the rich man as he continued on into the streets.

The idea felt powerful, perhaps even scary, yet exciting at the same time.

If Arkad had started poor...
  If he had learned something...
    Could *they* learn it too?

Daria sat up straight. Her eyes were bright now.

"Let's ask him," she said.

Karim almost choked. "Ask Arkad? The richest man in the city? Just like that?"

"Why not?" Daria replied. "Think about it. Everyone says money 'follows rules.' If we keep doing what we're doing, we'll stay broke forever. I'm not okay with that."

Nadan felt his heart beat faster. He imagined walking up to Arkad.

Excuse me, richest man in Babylon, could you teach four clueless teenagers not to be disasters with money?

It sounded ridiculous.

But being broke forever sounded worse.

Bela grinned. "I'm in. We are already the Empty Pockets Club. Maybe we can become the Full Purses Club."

Karim shrugged. "If they throw us out, at least I'll have a story."

They all looked at Nadan.

He thought of the clay lion, the three coins, the feeling of his empty pouch at the end of every week, and the way Arkad had walked: calm, not chasing anything.

Nadan drew a slow breath and stepped forward. "Master Arkad?" he called.

Arkad turned. His eyes were steady, patient.

Nadan bowed his head. "My friends and I... we want to learn.

We are always broke. We work hard but end every week with empty pouches. I don't know what we're doing wrong."

Arkad studied him for a moment. "You are doing one thing right," he said. "You are asking."

Nadan swallowed. "Will you teach us?"

Arkad's expression softened just a touch. "I hold open talks in my courtyard. Come tomorrow. Listen. Think. If you are willing to change, you will learn."

Nadan nodded quickly. "We'll be there. Thank you"

Arkad gave a small smile and continued on his way, leaving Nadan standing with a strange new feeling in his chest: possibility.

Nadan rushed back to his friends.

Daria clapped her hands . "This is good. Arkad holds a kind of open talk in his courtyard every few days. My brother listens from outside the gate sometimes. He says people ask him questions, and Arkad answers and shares his wisdom."

"Tomorrow morning," Nadan said. "We'll go early and wait."

Bela groaned. "Early?"

"Yes, early," Daria said. "Or you can sleep in and stay poor."

Bela considered. "I'll be there."

That evening, as Nadan walked home, he passed the stall with the clay lion again. The little sculpture seemed to stare back at him.

"Two coins," the seller reminded him. "Think how good it would look in your room."

It *would* look good. But tomorrow they were going to see Arkad. They were going to ask how to stop being broke. It felt wrong to show up with only one coin left.

Nadan put his hand on the lion, then slowly pulled it back.

"Not today," he said. "Maybe another time."

The seller rolled his eyes. "Kids," he muttered.

Nadan walked away with his three coins still in his pouch. For once, **not spending** felt… interesting. Like the start of something.

That night he lay awake, listening to the sounds of the city calming down, and imagined what he would ask Arkad. A strange thought came to him:

What if the problem isn't how much I earn, but what I do with it?

He fell asleep wondering what the richest man in Babylon would say.

Tomorrow, he'd find out.

2

The Secret of the First Coin

The next morning, Babylon was already buzzing when Nadan left his house.

Women carried water jars on their heads, merchants dragged open their shop shutters, and the sun was just climbing high enough to turn everything yellow and gold. Nadan walked quickly, his belt pouch bumping against his side.

Inside were **three coins**.

He kept touching them to make sure they were still there.

He reached Arkad's street and saw a crowd already gathering around a wide wooden gate. People leaned against the walls, talking, waiting. Some wore fine robes. Others looked like workers and messengers, dusty from the road.

Daria waved him over. "You're late."

"I'm early for me," Nadan said. Bela and Karim stood beside her, half-asleep.

Bela yawned. "If this man doesn't show up, I want compensation."

"In what?" Daria asked. "Regret?"

The wooden gate creaked open.

A servant stepped out. "Arkad will speak soon," he announced. "You may enter. Be respectful."

The crowd pushed forward. Nadan and his friends squeezed through and found a place near one of the stone pillars in the courtyard.

Arkad's house was big but not flashy. The courtyard had a low pool in the middle with still water and some plants around the edges. Benches lined the walls. People sat where they could, or stood wherever there was space.

Nadan's heart thumped. *He's really going to teach us,* he thought.

After a few moments, Arkad himself walked in.

He wore a plain but clean robe and simple sandals. Nothing on him shouted, *I am the richest man in Babylon.* Yet, he exuded a quiet calm that hinted at tremendous wealth and wisdom.

Everyone went quiet as he entered.

Arkad sat on a raised stone seat and looked around the circle of faces.

"Friends," he said, in a calm, normal voice, "why have you come?"

A man with a trade belt spoke first. "To learn how to get more gold, Arkad."

Laughter rippled through the crowd.

Arkad smiled. "If I could simply toss gold at you," he said, "this courtyard would be even more crowded. But you do not truly want my gold. You want to know how to make and keep your own. Yes?"

Heads nodded. Nadan felt Daria shift beside him.

Arkad's eyes moved slowly around the courtyard.

"Who here," he asked, "works hard, yet often feels poor?"

Almost every hand went up, including Nadan's.

"Good," Arkad said. "You are honest. That is the first step."

He rested his hands on his knees. "I was once like you. I worked long hours writing on clay tablets for others. At the end of each month, my pouch was as flat as the poorest man's.

Then one day I asked myself a simple question:

If others can become rich in this city, why not me?

He pointed toward the gates, toward the busy streets beyond.

"Babylon is not a cruel master," he said. "It pays those who know how to work with money. So I looked for answers, and I found teachers. Today, I will share the first lesson they gave me."

Nadan leaned forward. *Here it comes,* he thought.

Arkad held up one finger.

"From this day on, keep **at least one coin out of every ten** you receive."

There was a short silence.

"That's it?" someone blurted out.

Arkad laughed, not offended at all. "Yes. That is it. The first rule is that simple."

"But I already don't have enough!" called a woman near the back. "If I keep one out of ten, how will I pay for everything?"

"Exactly," added another man. "Everything I earn has a job. Food, rent, clothes, debts. There is nothing left."

Arkad nodded as if he had heard the same thing a hundred times. He probably had.

"When I first heard this rule," he said, "I thought the same. I told my teacher, 'I am not a child. I do not waste my coins.' He did not argue with me. He simply asked: 'Have you been able to keep any of your earnings so far?'"

He spread his hands. "I had to admit the truth. I had not."

The courtyard stayed quiet. Nadan felt his face grow warm. *This is me,* he thought. *This is all of us.*

Arkad looked at the crowd. "If you always feel like your money disappears, then whatever you are doing now is not working. So try something different. Keep one coin out of ten for yourself. You are allowed to pay yourself."

He let that sink in.

"You will say, 'But I cannot cut anything!'" Arkad continued. "I say, you already cut something. You cut your own future. You pay everyone else, bakers, landlords, cloth-makers, but you pay nothing to the one person who will live with your decisions the longest: you."

He leaned forward.

"Start paying yourself."

Nadan swallowed. The idea hit him like a gentle punch.

He imagined his coins marching away each month to everyone else, while future Nadan sat on the floor in an empty house, watching them go.

A man near the front raised his hand. "And once we keep this one coin out of ten," he said, "what do we do with it?"

"Later," Arkad said. "First, learn to keep it. If you cannot hold on to money, no trick or investment will save you."

He looked around the courtyard.

"For a whole month," he said, "try this: every time you are paid, set aside at least ten percent. Do not spend it. Not on sweets. Not on new sandals. Not on gifts. Not even on small 'emergencies' that are actually poor planning."

Some people laughed bitterly. Others looked uncomfortable.

"If you cannot survive on ninety percent of what you earn," Arkad said softly, "you also cannot survive on a little more. But if you try, you will see: you can."

He sat back.

"That is all for today," he said. "Learn to keep the first part of your money. When you return, we will discuss what to do with it."

The crowd started buzzing with whispers.

"That's it?" Karim whispered to Nadan. "We got up early for *that?*"

"What were you expecting?" Daria replied. "A hidden vault under his house?"

Bela frowned. "I was expecting something more... impressive."

Nadan stayed silent. He could still hear the sentence in his head:

You pay everyone else, but not yourself.

As people left the courtyard, Arkad spoke with some of them individually. Nadan watched him, then took a breath.

"I'm going to ask him a question," he said.

Daria's eyebrows shot up. "Now?"

"When else?" Nadan said.

He walked toward the front while the crowd thinned. His hands felt sweaty. Arkad turned to leave, then noticed him.

"Yes, young man?" Arkad asked.

Nadan almost forgot how to talk. "Sir, what if... what if we're not earning that much? I'm just an assistant. One coin out of ten feels like a lot."

Arkad's eyes were kind but sharp. "How many coins do you earn in a month, roughly?"

Nadan told him.

"And how many do you usually have left at the end of the month?" Arkad asked.

Nadan knew the answer. "Zero."

"Then," Arkad said calmly, "keeping one out of ten means you will end with more than you do now."

Nadan opened his mouth, then closed it.

Arkad put a hand on his shoulder. "You are young. If you learn this now, you will be ahead of almost everyone. Start with one in ten. When that becomes normal, you may keep more. But start."

Nadan nodded slowly. "Yes, sir."

Arkad's hand squeezed his shoulder once, then he turned away to speak with someone else.

Nadan returned to his friends.

"Well?" Bela asked.

"He told me to do exactly what he already said," Nadan replied.

Karim groaned. "Great."

But Nadan felt different. Somehow, hearing it aimed directly at him made it heavier, more real.

They walked back through the city, the four of them in a row.

"So... what do we do?" Karim asked.

Daria answered quickly. "We test it. One coin out of ten. For a month."

Bela pulled a face. "A whole month? What if I need sandals?"

"You have sandals," Daria said.

"They're ugly," Bela said.

"They're fine," Daria replied. "And even if they aren't, future you will not care what shoes you wore this year. He will care whether you are broke or not."

They crossed a busy street. Nadan dodged a cart and shook his head.

"What if Arkad is wrong?" he asked.

Daria actually laughed. "He's the richest man in Babylon. If he's wrong, I want to be wrong like him."

Karim kicked a pebble. "What if we try it and it doesn't work?"

"Then we'll still be broke," Bela said. "Which is where we are now. So we lose nothing."

Nadan thought about his three coins again. "One in ten," he repeated softly.

They reached their usual palm tree and sat in the shade.

"Let's make it official," Daria said. "Empty Pockets Club is dead. From now on, we're... what?"

Bela raised his hands dramatically. "The Full Purses Society!"

Karim shook his head. "Too long."

"First Coins," Nadan suggested. "Because we're keeping the first part for ourselves."

Daria considered. "I like it."

She leaned forward.

"Rules of the First Coins," she said. "Rule one: Every time we get paid, we take at least ten percent and set it aside for ourselves. Non-negotiable."

"Rule two," Bela added. "We meet here once a week and check if we actually did it. If someone breaks the rule, they have to admit it."

Karim pointed a finger at him. "You are definitely going to be the first one to break it."

"Probably," Bela said cheerfully. "Which is why we need the rule."

Nadan smiled despite his nerves.

"Agreed," he said. "We all follow it for a month. Then we go back to Arkad and see what the next lesson is."

They put their hands together in the middle, like they had done when they started the Empty Pockets Club, only this time the mood was different. Less joking, more serious.

"First Coins," Daria said. "One, two, three……"

"First Coins!" they shouted.

A passing farmer stared at them, confused. They burst out laughing.

The real test began that same week.

Nadan's pay day came on a hot afternoon. His master, the scribe, handed him a small cloth bag.

"You worked well," the man said. "Don't waste it."

"I'll try," Nadan said, thinking of Arkad.

He walked out of the workshop and into the street. The bag

felt heavier than usual, not because there were more coins inside, but because they now had a **job**.

Under the shade of a doorway, he opened the bag and counted. Then, heart beating a little faster, he did something he had never done before.

He **took out one coin in ten** and slid it into a separate pouch he had tied tightly inside his belt, where it would be hard to reach.

"This part is not for spending," he told himself quietly. "This is mine. For future me."

He closed both pouches and stood there for a moment, feeling strangely proud and strangely nervous all at once.

The rest of the coins still felt like "normal money", money that would quickly vanish on food, little treats, and small "needs" that weren't always truly needed.

But that one-tenth… it felt different. Protected.

That evening at home, temptation showed up almost immediately. His younger brother begged him to go to the market and buy honey cakes. His mother reminded him that he needed a new belt soon. His friend stopped by and suggested they rent seats near the musicians in the square.

All three things sounded fun. All three could eat up his money.

FIRST COINS

For the first time in his life, Nadan looked at his coins and thought in two parts:

- **The part I can spend now.**
- **The part I am not allowed to touch.**

He paid for some simple food, skipped the honey cakes, and told his friend he'd listen to the music from farther back where it was free.

Was it painful? A little.

But as he lay in bed that night, he thought of the hidden pouch inside his belt. There was still money in there. Money that belonged to his future.

It felt... good.

The others were having their own battles.

Bela almost broke the rule on the very first day.

A seller roamed through his street with a basket of roasted nuts, and the smell drove Bela crazy. He reached into his pouch automatically, then stopped, remembering the rule.

"Ninety percent, Bela," he whispered to himself. "You can spend ninety percent. But not the first part."

He did some fast mental counting, grumbled, and bought a

smaller handful than usual. It wasn't easy, but he still had his First Coins safe.

Daria, who already spent less than the others, found that the rule did not hurt as much as she feared. She cut back on small things, an extra cup of sweet drink here, a piece of cloth there, and survived just fine.

Karim struggled the most. He owed small amounts to several people, old borrowing that had piled up. Each one wanted to be paid.

"Tell them you will pay them," Daria told him, "but that you must first pay yourself. Then make slow, steady payments from the rest."

"They'll be angry," Karim said.

"They'll be more angry," Daria replied, "if you stay broke forever."

A week later, they met again under the palm tree.

Nadan arrived first. He sat with his back against the trunk, took out the small inner pouch, and emptied it carefully into his hand.

Several coins clinked together, more than he was used to seeing lying still in front of him.

He smiled.

Bela arrived next, then Daria, then Karim, all looking nervous.

"All right," Daria said. "Confession time. Who kept the rule?"

They looked at one another, then, one by one, they opened their "first coin" pouches and showed what they had.

The amounts were small. Nothing that would impress anyone in the market. But for them, it was different.

It was **money that had survived a week.**

They had paid themselves.

Bela let out a low whistle. "I've never kept this much for more than a day," he admitted.

Karim poked his little pile. "It's not much," he said.

"It is more than zero," Daria replied. "And it is not the only week. Imagine this every week, for a whole year."

Nadan did the maths in his head. His eyes widened.

"That's... actually a lot," he said.

"For the first time," Daria said quietly, "our money is not just passing through our hands. Some of it is staying."

They sat there, each looking at their small piles, feeling a new kind of power growing.

Not the power of suddenly being rich, but the power of **not being controlled** by every little want and impulse.

"Do you think Arkad will really tell us what to do next?" Bela asked.

"He said he would," Nadan said. "Once we can keep it."

Daria nodded. "Then we keep doing this. Week after week. Until it feels normal."

Karim sighed. "Goodbye, extra honey cakes."

"Goodbye, broke, stressed-out future me," Daria replied.

They laughed.

For the first time since they had declared themselves the Empty Pockets Club, their name felt wrong. Their pockets were not full yet, but they weren't empty either.

Something was starting.

And somewhere, in a courtyard not far away, the richest man in Babylon knew that a few young minds had taken the first, most important step:

They had learned the secret of the first coin.

3

Coins That Grow While You Sleep

A month later, the courtyard was even more crowded. Word had spread that Arkad was giving lessons again. This time, the crowd spilled out through the gate and into the street. People packed in shoulder to shoulder, from grey-bearded traders to teenage messengers still carrying satchels.

Nadan, Bela, Daria, and Karim squeezed themselves into almost the same spot as last time.

"How much do you think he has?" Bela whispered, peering toward the house. "Like… actual coins."

"A mountain," Karim said.

"A warehouse," Daria said.

"A system," Nadan said quietly.

They all looked at him.

"What?" Bela asked.

Nadan shrugged. "Last time, he didn't give us gold. He gave us a rule. It's the rules that make the mountain."

Bela opened his mouth, then closed it. "Okay, that was annoyingly wise," he admitted.

Before they could argue more, Arkad walked into the courtyard.

Once again, the noise dropped without anyone asking for silence. He sat on the stone seat, looked around at the sea of faces, and smiled.

"Friends," he said, "who here *tried* keeping one coin out of ten?"

Hands went up all around the courtyard, including four hands by the palm-tree teenagers.

"Good," Arkad said. "Who found it hard?"

Almost the same hands went up again.

Laughter rolled through the place.

Arkad nodded. "Money is like a wild animal at first. It wants to run in every direction. You must train it. Now tell me: did anyone *manage* to keep their first coins?"

Voices rose:

"I did."
  "Some of it."
  "Not all the time, but yes."

Arkad held up a hand for quiet.

"If you kept even a little," he said, "you have already done more for your future than most people ever do. Now your money is ready for the second lesson."

Nadan's chest tightened with excitement. *Here we go,* he thought.

Arkad turned his palm upward, as if holding something invisible.

"Money that just sits still is lazy," he said. "It must be put to work. A coin you save is a good start. A coin that earns another coin is even better."

He looked around.

"Imagine you plant a date seed," he said. "If you eat the seed, it is gone. If you plant it, in time it becomes a tree. That tree gives many more seeds. If you plant those as well, soon you have a whole grove that feeds you every year. Money can do that. A single coin, wisely placed, can grow into many coins that keep on working for you."

Bela nudged Nadan. "I like this seed," he whispered.

Arkad continued. "When you put your saved coins to good use, they become like seeds. You plant them in the right soil, and they grow quietly while you sleep."

He glanced at the crowd. "And the fruit they give contains more seeds. Those seeds can be planted too. Soon one small planting becomes a grove, and a grove becomes an orchard. In time, the harvest from that orchard will feed you, your family, and perhaps even your children's children."

He lifted a finger. "But plant your seeds in barren ground, and nothing grows. Plant them where thieves or storms can destroy them, and you lose everything. Your coins are no different. Choose the soil with care."

"So we should just… lend money to people?" someone called out.

"Sometimes," Arkad said. "Or join their business. Or buy part of something that earns. But listen carefully."

He leaned forward.

"If you send your coins to work with foolish people, they will not come back. They will die in the field and leave you poorer than before."

Murmurs ran through the crowd.

Arkad held up his hand. "I once made this mistake. When I was young and had just started saving, I was eager to grow my coins quickly. A friend of mine, a brickmaker, told me he had a wonderful idea."

Nadan's ears pricked up. This was the story he'd heard hints about: the brickmaker and the jewels.

"He said," Arkad went on, "'Let us buy rare jewels from a far land. We will take them to the city and sell them for a great profit.' It sounded exciting. I gave him my savings. He gave my money to a man who claimed to be a dealer in jewels."

"Let me guess," Bela muttered.

"When the jewels arrived," Arkad said, "we took them to a proper jeweller. The man laughed until tears ran down his face. 'These are coloured glass,' he said. 'Pretty, but worth almost nothing.'"

The courtyard groaned in sympathy. A few people laughed bitterly, recognising their own mistakes.

Arkad smiled at his younger self. "My coins were gone. I had trusted a brickmaker about jewels. That was not fair to him or to my money."

He let the silence sit for a moment.

"From then on," he said, "I promised myself: I will only send my coins to work in fields I understand, or with people who know that field very well and have proved they are careful."

He tapped his knee for emphasis.

"To make money grow, you need **two things**:

1. Coins you do not spend.
2. Wise places to put them."

Arkad sat back. "Today, I want each of you to ask yourself: *What work could my saved coins do?* Not crazy tricks. Not gambling. Real work that brings regular returns."

He looked toward the teenagers' corner, not because he knew about their little club, but because their faces were wide open and focused in a way he liked.

"For some," he said, "it might be lending to a reliable merchant who repays with a little extra each month. For others, joining a trusted craftsman to buy tools or materials, sharing in the profits. Whatever it is, start small and start **wise**."

A woman raised her hand. "How do we know if it's wise?" she asked.

Arkad smiled. "You ask questions. Many questions. You check whether the person has succeeded before. You think about the worst that could happen. If, after all that, it seems too good to be true, it probably is."

He paused, looking around the circle.

"Gold flees from the man who tries to force it to grow too fast. It happily stays with the one who is patient and careful."

He nodded, as if to himself. "That is enough for one day. Go back to your homes. Look at the coins you kept. Ask: how can I put them to safe work?"

The crowd slowly unfolded into movement and noise.

"Well?" Bela said as they filed out into the street. "Time to find a jewel dealer with amazing offers?"

Karim snorted. "Only if he also sells flying donkeys."

Daria was quiet, thinking. "He said start small," she murmured. "Safe, steady returns. Not exciting."

"Exciting is overrated," Nadan said. "I just don't want to go back to zero. Ever."

They walked through Babylon with the lesson hanging in the air around them.

The city suddenly looked different to Nadan. Every shop, every cart, every stall represented someone's money at work.

The man selling bread had bought flour and paid for a stall. The woman selling dyed cloth had invested in colour and fabric. Even the man with a tiny basket of dates had taken a risk: would he sell them all before they spoiled?

Their money is working, Nadan thought. *Mine is still learning how.*

They met under the palm tree that afternoon, like always.

Daria drew a circle in the dust with a stick. "We have two problems," she said.

"Only two?" Bela joked.

She ignored him. "First problem: we finally have *some* saved coins, but not a huge amount. Second problem: we don't know great business opportunities."

Karim lay on his back and stared at the leaves. "And third problem," he added, "I am allergic to losing my money."

"That's not a problem," Nadan said. "That's a survival instinct."

Daria drew four small piles in the dust. "Let's think. What kind of work could our coins do *now*, at our age?"

"Gambling on dice," Bela said.

Daria glared.

He held up his hands. "Kidding. Mostly."

Karim rolled onto his side. "We could lend money to people," he said. "Like little mini-bankers."

"Lending to who?" Daria asked. "If they don't pay us back, our first lesson dies."

"What about people we know?" Bela suggested. "Like my cousin who always needs a little to go to the fights."

"The cousin who never has money?" Daria said. "Great business partner."

Bela sighed. "Fine. No."

Nadan thought about the craftsmen he saw each day near the scribe's workshop. "What about someone who already knows how to make more money," he said slowly, "but needs a little extra to grow their work?"

"Like who?" Daria asked.

Nadan frowned in concentration. After a moment, his face brightened.

"The shield-maker," he said. "You know, the one near the inner gate."

Karim sat up. "The one with the loud hammer?"

"That one," Nadan said. "He's busy all the time. People are always picking up orders. Sometimes he sends his apprentice to borrow money to buy more bronze. I've seen it."

Daria's eyes narrowed thoughtfully. "Do you think he pays people back?"

"I've never heard anyone complain," Nadan said. "And if he didn't, he wouldn't be able to borrow anymore. Word travels fast."

Bela perked up. "So we give him coins to buy bronze, he makes shields, sells them, and pays us back with extra?"

"Exactly," Nadan said. "Our coins help him earn more. He shares a bit of that with us. That's… putting coins to work, right?"

Daria couldn't hide her smile. "That's… actually good," she said.

Karim looked nervous. "What if the price of bronze suddenly changes? Or soldiers stop buying shields?"

"Then we lose," Daria said simply. "That's why we'll start small. Test it. If it works, we can slowly increase."

Bela rubbed his hands together. "So we're starting a tiny investment club."

"We already started it," Nadan said. "We gave it a name: First Coins. This is just the next step."

The next day, they went to see the shield-maker.

His workshop was impossible to miss.

CLANG. CLANG. CLANG.

The sound of metal on metal rang out into the street. Sparks flew as the shield-maker hammered hot bronze against a curved form. His arms were thick, and his face was streaked with sweat and soot.

When he saw the four teenagers standing there, he raised an eyebrow.

"Yes?" he said, not stopping his work.

"Sir," Nadan began, suddenly feeling very small, "we... we have a question."

"Then ask it loud," the man grunted. "The hammer doesn't move quietly."

Daria stepped forward. "We've seen that you sometimes borrow money to buy bronze," she said. "If someone lent you a small amount, would you be willing to pay them back with a little extra after you sold the shields?"

The shield-maker paused mid-swing. The hot metal hissed as he let it rest on the anvil.

"You want to lend *me* money?" he asked, wiping his forehead with his arm.

"Yes, sir," Daria said. "But only if it's useful for you. And only if you're sure you can pay it back."

Bela muttered under his breath, "Smooth."

The man chuckled. "Children trying to be bankers. Babylon gets stranger every year."

He picked up a jug of water, drank, and thought for a moment.

"I do borrow sometimes," he said slowly. "Bronze sellers don't wait, soldiers don't wait, but my payments come when orders are finished. Lending helps me bridge the gap."

He looked them over, one by one. "How much are we talking about?"

They glanced at one another. Their combined savings weren't huge, and they weren't about to risk it all.

Nadan named a modest amount that represented just a slice of what each of them had.

The shield-maker nodded. "That much," he said, "would buy enough bronze for maybe two extra shields. The profit from those would be more than your loan. I could pay you back in… let's say one month, with an extra…" He considered, then named a fair amount.

Daria didn't smile yet. "How often have you borrowed and repaid like this?" she asked.

The man grinned. "You've been listening to Arkad, haven't you?"

They blinked.

He laughed. "You have his look, cautious and annoying." He gestured toward the street. "I have borrowed from traders and neighbours for years. Ask them if I don't pay."

He listed three names they recognised from the market. All were respectable. None were known as fools.

"That's good enough for me," Nadan said quietly.

"Not for me," Daria replied automatically. "Two more questions: what happens if there's some problem and you can't pay in a month? And when would you need the money?"

The shield-maker seemed to enjoy this conversation. "If something slows me down," he said, "I still have shields and bronze. They are worth something. Worst case, I sell them cheaper, but I can still repay. As for when I need the money—" he pointed to the nearly empty bronze bucket "—yesterday."

Bela whispered, "This man speaks my language."

The shield-maker wiped his hands. "Tell you what. You bring me your coins first thing tomorrow morning. I'll scratch your names and the amount into a clay tablet, with the date and the payment I owe you. When I repay, we'll break the tablet. Agreed?"

They looked at each other. Nadan felt a mixture of fear and excitement. This was it: the moment their coins would go out to "work."

Daria nodded slowly. "Agreed," she said.

"Then go." The hammer rose again. "I finish this shield before the sun sleeps."

CLANG.

That night, Nadan lay awake again.

What if we lose it? he thought.

He imagined Arkad's voice: *Start small. Test first.*

They weren't risking everything. Just enough to see if the idea worked.

He also thought about something Arkad hadn't said directly but was easy to see: **there is no way to grow money without some risk.**

The trick was choosing **smart risk**, not crazy risk.

He placed his hand over his pouch, feeling the familiar weight of the coins. Tomorrow, some of them would leave. But if the shield-maker was as solid as he seemed, they would come back... with friends.

Coins that grow while you sleep, Nadan thought.

He finally drifted off imagining his money walking off like small workers, carrying tools.

The next day, the First Coins club handed over their agreed amount to the shield-maker.

True to his word, he baked a clay tablet, pressed their names and numbers into it, and let it dry in the sun.

"Your money will come back stronger," he said. "Unless Babylon falls, in which case we have bigger problems."

A month had never felt so long.

Every time Nadan passed the workshop and heard the hammer, he wondered if those blows were hitting *his* coins too, bending them into shields.

Bela swung by the shop almost every other day, pretending he just "happened to be in the area," which fooled nobody.

Karim worried constantly. "What if soldiers stop needing shields?" he asked for the fifth time.

"There are always wars," Bela said darkly.

"That doesn't make me feel better," Karim replied.

Daria kept a simple record in a clay tablet she carried. "Even if this goes well," she reminded them, "we do not jump into the next shiny thing. Slow, steady, safe. We're not trying to get rich in a week."

"Speak for yourself," Bela said, but only half-seriously.

Exactly one month later, they stood once again in the echoing workshop.

The shield-maker laid their tablet on the anvil.

"You picked a good month to test this," he said. "The king's guards ordered extra shields. Your bronze helped me fill the order faster."

He handed back their original amount **plus** the extra he had promised.

Using the blunt side of his hammer, he struck the tablet. It cracked neatly into pieces.

"Paid in full," he said.

For a heartbeat, they just stared at the coins in his hand.

They weren't imagining it. Their money had left… and come back **with more money.**

Nadan's fingers trembled slightly as he accepted his share.

"Thank you," Daria said. "We appreciate your honesty."

The shield-maker shrugged, pleased. "You helped me earn more. Why would I cheat the people I can do honest business with again?"

Bela grinned. "Can we lend you more?"

Daria elbowed him. "Slow down."

The man laughed. "Maybe. But be wise." He lifted his hammer again. "Plenty of people in Babylon would happily take your coins and give you nothing back. Gamble houses, slick talkers, 'rare jewel' dealers…" He shook his head. "You chose a man whose work you can see and hear."

CLANG.

The hammer came down, ending the conversation.

Under the palm tree that afternoon, their coins sat in four neat piles, bigger than before.

"So," Bela said, "what did we just prove?"

"That this works," Karim said softly. "This isn't a story. It's real."

Daria nodded.

"We learned three things," she said, drawing marks in the dust.

"First: Saving on its own is good, but saving plus **wise investing** is better. Our coins can go out and work, then come home."

"Second: Not every opportunity is equal. Lending to a shield-maker for bronze is different from betting on dice or trusting a stranger selling jewels."

"Third: It feels amazing," Bela added, "and I want to do it again."

They laughed.

Then Nadan remembered something Arkad had said: *Money that grows makes its owner eager for more growth. But greed can make a wise man foolish.*

He looked at his friends.

"Before we rush," he said, "maybe we should set some rules for how we invest."

Daria smiled. "Agreed. New rules for the First Coins."

She etched them into the clay tablet:

1. **We only invest money we have already saved.** No borrowing to gamble.
2. **We start small.** Test people and plans before trusting them with more.

3. **We only invest with people who know their trade and have a good reputation.**
4. **We never put all our savings into one thing.**
5. **If something promises huge returns very quickly, we assume it's a trap until proved otherwise.**

"That last one needs to be in big letters," Karim said.

"I'll decorate it," Bela offered. "With skulls."

They all laughed again, but there was a seriousness beneath it now. The numbers in their pouches might be small, but the direction of their lives had changed.

They weren't just *workers* anymore.

They were becoming **owners,** of decisions, of habits, and now, slowly, of money that worked for them.

Nadan closed his hand around his coins and felt their familiar weight.

"Coins that grow while you sleep," he murmured.

Daria heard him. "Exactly," she said. "And this is only the beginning. Arkad mentioned something else, remember?"

"What?" Bela asked.

"Guarding your money from loss," Daria said. "We got lucky

with our first investment. But sooner or later, someone will offer us something that sounds too perfect."

Karim shivered. "The brickmaker's jewels."

"Right," Daria said. "The next lesson is how not to fall for our own greed."

Nadan looked toward the city, where, somewhere, Arkad was probably teaching another group. Their path was clear:

- Save a part of all they earned.
- Make those saved coins work.
- Learn how to protect them from their own mistakes.

For the first time in his life, the future didn't look like a foggy, scary place.

It looked like a city full of jobs their money hadn't done yet.

4

The Deal That Looked Too Perfect

Two months after their first visit to Arkad, the First Coins club was starting to feel…different.

Their clothes were still plain. Their houses were still simple. No one would look at them and say, "Ah yes, those are the young financial geniuses of Babylon."

But inside their pouches, things had changed.

- They still **saved** one coin out of every ten.
- They had made **two more small loans** to the shield-maker, all repaid on time with profit.
- Their savings piles were slowly, steadily growing.

It wasn't dramatic. It was something better: **steady**.

Then temptation showed up.

THE DEAL THAT LOOKED TOO PERFECT

It began with Bela, naturally.

He burst under the palm tree one afternoon, almost vibrating with excitement.

"You are not going to believe what I found," he said.

Daria didn't look impressed. "A way to spend all your savings in one day?"

"Better," Bela said. "A way to *double* them."

Karim groaned in advance. "This already sounds bad."

Nadan watched Bela carefully. "Explain."

Bela sat down, trying and failing to look calm.

"You know my cousin Mahir?" he began.

"The one who's always broke and always 'about to be rich'?" Daria said.

"That's unfair," Bela protested. "Sometimes he's just broke."

Daria folded her arms. "Go on."

"Mahir's been working with a man from Tyre," Bela said. "A trader. This man buys fine purple cloth from the coast and sells it here to nobles. It's very expensive, very rare. Mahir says the trader has more demand than he can supply."

He paused for effect.

"So," Bela continued, "the trader is offering something special. For a limited time, if someone lends him silver, he'll repay **double** in just two months. Because he can buy much more cloth with our money, sell it, and share the huge profit."

Karim sat up straighter despite himself. "Double?"

"Double," Bela said. "Two months."

Daria looked suspicious. "Why only 'for a limited time'?"

"Because he only needs money for his next big shipment," Bela said. "Then he'll have enough to stand on his own."

Nadan frowned. "How do you know all this?"

"I told you, Mahir is helping him," Bela said. "He told me everything. He even said he's putting in his own money."

"That doesn't comfort me," Daria muttered.

Bela leaned forward, eyes shining. "Look, we've been careful. We've been slow. That's good. But Arkad also said money can work for us. This is a chance for it to work *hard*. We put in our savings, two months later we have **twice as much**. Imagine how many safe, boring investments we could do after that!"

Karim chewed his lip. "It does sound… incredible."

"That's the problem," Daria said quietly. "It sounds incredible."

She picked up a stick and drew a big circle in the dust.

"Let's remember what we wrote down," she said. "Rule five: *If something promises huge returns very quickly, we assume it's a trap until proved otherwise.*"

Bela threw up his hands. "You all act like every good thing is a trap."

Nadan stayed silent. He could feel the pull of the idea in his chest. Double. Two months. It was huge. With that much, they could—

He cut off the thought.

"Have you met the trader yourself?" Nadan asked.

"Yes," Bela said. "He's impressive. Confident. He dresses well, speaks well. He has real purple cloth. I touched it. And I know at least one man who already lent him money, and that man's shipment came back with profit."

"Who?" Daria asked.

"A spice seller in the market," Bela said. "You know, the one with the missing tooth? He told me he's making 'the deal of his life.'"

"That does not prove much," Daria said, but her voice was less sure now.

Karim turned to Nadan. "What do you think?"

Nadan looked at Bela.

"Can we see this trader ourselves?" he asked. "Ask questions?"

Bela nodded eagerly. "Of course. Mahir said he'd be happy to meet us."

Daria sighed. "Fine. We'll talk to him. **But just talk.**" She gave Bela a hard look. "No handing over coins because he smiles nicely."

Bela held a hand to his chest. "Would I do that?"

"Yes," all three of them said in unison.

The trader's stall was near the inner market, where the richer customers liked to shop.

Purple cloth really did hang there, deep, dark, almost glowing in the sun. Nadan had never seen anything like it up close. It looked like something only a prince would wear.

The trader himself matched his goods. He had neatly trimmed hair, a short beard, and rings on his fingers. His smile was smooth and quick.

"Friends of Mahir," he said warmly when Bela introduced them.

"Welcome."

He offered them water and dates before they even asked anything. The purple cloth swayed gently behind him, like a rich curtain.

Nadan felt slightly off-balance. Everything about this man was polished.

"We heard you sometimes borrow money to buy more cloth," Daria said, skipping over the small talk. "And that you pay back double in two months."

The trader nodded, as if this was the most normal thing in the world.

"Correct," he said. "My trade is simple. Purple cloth from the coast, nobles here pay very well. But the cloth sellers there demand payment upfront, and I cannot always move fast enough on my own. So I let others join my success for a time. They lend silver, I buy more cloth, we all profit."

He spoke smoothly, with the rhythm of someone who had told this story many times.

Karim shifted uneasily. "What if the ship sinks?" he blurted.

The trader laughed lightly. "Ships rarely sink on this route, my friend. I have been trading for years. Of course there is some risk in all things. But the profit is so great that it is worth it."

Nadan remembered Arkad's words: *Ask many questions. Think about the worst that could happen.*

"What if the nobles stop wanting purple?" Nadan asked. "Or a new trader arrives and sells it cheaper?"

The man's smile flickered for half a second, then returned.

"Purple has always been desired by kings and nobles," he said smoothly. "It is a sign of power and wealth. That does not change. As for other traders, competition exists, but my contacts are strong. I assure you, my young friends, I know my business."

He sounded confident. Too confident.

"How much have you personally invested in this next shipment?" Daria asked.

The trader hesitated slightly.

"Much," he said. "But as a trader, I also must stay flexible. That is why I invite others to join. You get a share of large profits without managing the details."

Daria's eyes narrowed just a little.

Bela jumped in. "We heard that a spice seller already made money with you."

"Ah, Kazim!" the trader said quickly, latching onto the name.

"Yes, yes. He is thrilled. Tell me, do you want to be like him, or do you want to stand on the side while others grow rich?"

It was a sharp line, thrown like a hook directly at their pride.

Nadan felt it sting. *Do you want to be the smart ones or the scared ones?* the question seemed to say.

"We will think about it," Daria said firmly, before anyone else could speak.

The trader's eyes cooled just a little. "Of course," he said. "But understand, opportunities do not wait forever. The ship leaves in three days. Decide quickly, or watch others take the chance."

Bela looked pained. "Three days?"

"Three days," the trader repeated. "And then your money could be growing on the sea while you sleep."

He smiled one more time, and it was so confident, so smooth, that for a moment Nadan almost believed the future was already written: they would give him money, the ship would sail, and they would all return rich.

Under the palm tree, the argument started almost immediately.

"We're doing it," Bela said. "Right? We're doing it. This is exactly what Arkad was talking about, coins going out to work."

"No," Daria said. "This is exactly what Arkad was *warning* us about, trying to force our money to grow too fast."

"But the profit—" Karim began.

"—is what's blinding you," Daria snapped. "Double in two months? While we do nothing? Does that sound like the shield-maker, carefully hammering metal all day? Or does it sound like magic?"

Bela threw his hands up. "Not everyone earns slowly, Daria! Some trades are more profitable. That doesn't make them evil."

Nadan stayed quiet, running the conversation with Arkad through his mind.

If you send your coins to work with foolish people, they will not come back.
   Gold flees from the man who tries to force it to grow too fast.

"I don't think the trader is foolish," Bela went on. "He knows his business. He has real cloth. He helped Kazim. This is not gambling."

Daria's voice softened slightly. "I'm not saying he's a crook. I'm saying: if something goes wrong, will he still protect *our* coins? Or will he protect himself first?"

Silence.

Karim sighed. "We don't know."

Nadan finally spoke. "Arkad lost his savings by trusting a brickmaker about jewels," he said. "Who are *we* trusting here?"

"A trader about trading," Bela said quickly. "That's fair."

"But do we know his history?" Nadan pressed. "Has he repaid people for years like the shield-maker? Or is he just new and shiny?"

Bela hesitated. "We know about Kazim."

"One person," Daria said. "Is that enough?"

They went back and forth until the sun started dropping.

In the end, they couldn't agree.

Bela wanted in. Daria wanted out. Karim was torn in half. Nadan's stomach twisted every time he pictured handing over his coins.

Finally Nadan said, "Tomorrow, I'm going to ask Arkad one question. I'll find him in the courtyard or the street. I don't care. I want to hear *his* view on this kind of deal."

Daria nodded vigorously. "Good."

Bela shrugged. "Fine. Ask him. But we only have three days."

They didn't see Arkad in the courtyard the next morning. It was empty.

But Babylon is smaller than it looks when you're determined.

By midday, Nadan finally spotted him leaving a merchant's house with a sealed clay tablet in his hand.

"Sir!" Nadan called, running up to him.

Arkad's guard stepped in his way, but Arkad waved him aside.

"Yes, young scribe?" he said, recognising Nadan from the earlier talks.

Nadan's words tumbled out. "Sir, a trader is offering to double any silver we lend him in two months by buying purple cloth and selling it to nobles. My friend wants to invest. I'm not sure. Is this... wise?"

Arkad walked slowly, and Nadan matched his pace.

"Tell me," Arkad said, "what do you know about this trader?"

Nadan listed everything: the cloth, the stall, Kazim the spice seller, the confident smile, the "limited time" offer.

Arkad listened without interrupting.

When Nadan finished, Arkad asked one simple question:

"If you lost every coin you gave him, would you be surprised?"

"Yes," Nadan said honestly. "I think I would."

"Then you are not ready," Arkad replied.

Nadan blinked. "What do you mean?"

Arkad stopped walking and faced him.

"Sometimes," he said, "I give money knowing that I might lose it. I accept that risk. For example, if I support a friend trying a new venture, I might say, 'Here, try this. If it fails, I will not be angry.' That is a gift in disguise."

He raised a finger.

"But when I invest to grow my wealth, I do not want **surprises**. I want carefully measured risk. I want to think, 'If this goes wrong, I will be disappointed, but not shocked. I knew this could happen.'"

He looked Nadan in the eye.

"Promise of double in two months, with little explanation of the dangers? That smells like surprise."

Nadan swallowed. "So you would say no?"

"I would say this," Arkad replied. "If you truly understand this man's trade, his routes, his customers, his costs... if you have seen him handle loss well in the past... then perhaps. But from what you've told me, you are being asked to trust him mostly because he looks successful and speaks confidently."

He smiled slightly.

"Gold often runs toward confident voices," he said. "Then those voices disappear."

Nadan felt a cold little knot in his chest. "Thank you," he said quietly.

Arkad patted his shoulder. "You are doing well, young saver. Growing money is not a race. You have time. Better to be called cautious than to be called foolish and broke."

He turned and walked away, leaving Nadan alone in the busy street, surrounded by people who had no idea how loudly those words were echoing in his head.

Back under the palm tree, Nadan relayed everything Arkad had said.

Bela listened, jaw clenched.

"So that's it?" he said. "Because it's risky, we never take a chance? We just crawl slowly forever?"

"No," Nadan said calmly. "Because it's risky *and* we don't understand it, we pass."

Karim looked relieved. "I'm with Arkad," he said. "I hate surprises."

Daria nodded. "Me too."

Bela stared at them. "You're all afraid," he said.

"Maybe," Daria replied. "Or maybe we're just not desperate. We're already growing our money. Why throw away the one thing that's working for us?"

Silence stretched between them.

Finally Bela stood up. "You can do what you want," he said. "I can invest my own savings. It's my risk."

"That's true," Nadan said softly. "It is your risk. And we'll still be your friends even if we think it's a bad idea."

Bela looked at him, torn.

"Come with me," he said finally. "Just to watch. If you still disagree, I'll think again."

Daria rolled her eyes. "Fine. We'll watch you throw away your money."

They returned to the trader's stall together.

He welcomed them with the same polished smile. "I knew you'd be back," he said.

Bela stepped forward, hand on his pouch.

Before he could speak, Nadan interrupted.

"Sir," he said, "may I ask one more question?"

The trader's smile tightened a fraction. "Of course."

"If a storm sinks this shipment," Nadan said, "will you repay your lenders out of your own money anyway?"

The trader didn't hesitate. "The chance of such a storm is small," he said.

"That's not the question," Daria cut in. "The question is, if it happens, will you use your own wealth to protect ours?"

The trader's eyes cooled. Very slightly, but enough.

"Young people," he said smoothly, "no business is without risk. Those who join in the profit must also share in the danger. I am offering you a chance to earn greatly. That should be enough."

"Meaning," Daria said, "if the ship sinks, we lose everything and you lose… less."

The trader spread his hands. "I have many shipments. It would hurt me, of course. But I cannot promise what the sea will do. No one can."

Bela's fingers tightened on his pouch.

Nadan watched his friend's face. He could almost see the battle happening behind his eyes: greed vs fear, trust vs doubt.

"Three days," the trader reminded them. "Then the opportunity is gone."

Bela took a long, slow breath.

"Then let it be gone," he said quietly.

The trader blinked. "What?"

"I'm out," Bela said. "Thank you for your time."

He stepped back from the stall.

Daria let out a breath she'd been holding.

The trader tried once more. "You will regret this when your friends boast of their profit," he said.

"Maybe," Bela said. "Or maybe I'll still have my savings when their ship sinks."

He turned away. The others followed.

As they walked back through the market, Karim finally laughed, a nervous, shaky laugh that turned real.

"I thought you were going to do it," he told Bela.

"So did I," Bela admitted. "My hands hurt from not doing it."

Nadan smiled. "You just protected your future self from a surprise."

Daria nudged Bela's shoulder. "I'm proud of you," she said. "That took more courage than saying yes."

Bela grimaced. "It doesn't *feel* like courage. It feels like watching treasure sail away without me."

"Or watching a storm pass that you're not stuck in," Karim said.

They reached the palm tree and sat down.

Daria propped up her clay tablet and wrote at the top of a new page:

Lessons from the Deal That Looked Perfect

She listed them, reading aloud:

1. **Big promises + little explanation = danger.**
2. **If someone won't share your risk, don't give them your coins.**
3. **We would rather miss a profit than lose our savings.**
4. **Slow, steady growth beats quick, shaky growth.**

Bela watched her write, then nodded slowly.

"You know the worst part?" he said. "If this trader actually makes people rich, I'll feel stupid."

"You'll feel *fine*," Daria said. "Because you're playing a different game. You're not chasing every deal. You're building something."

Nadan looked at his friends, at the little tablet of rules, at the dust patterns under the palm tree where they'd once declared themselves the Empty Pockets Club.

They weren't that anymore.

They weren't rich. Not yet.

But they had something more important than a big pile of coins: they had **rules that protected their future**.

And that, he realised, is what Arkad meant by "guarding your treasure from loss."

5

A Home of Your Own

Rain in Babylon was rare.

Most days were hot and dry, but on this particular afternoon, the sky was low and grey and a light drizzle made the stone streets shine. People moved a little faster, pulling cloaks over their heads, ducking under awnings.

Nadan liked the rain. It made the city quieter.

He and his mother were patching a leak in the roof when she said something that stuck in his mind all day.

"These beams," she muttered, pressing mud into a crack, "they're not even ours. We fix them, we live under them, we worry about them. And in the end, the landlord still owns the house."

She caught herself and smiled at Nadan.

"Never mind me," she said. "I'm just tired. Pass me that clay."

But the words had already landed.

Not even ours.

Their house was small. One main room, a low sleeping area, a tiny space where his mother cooked. The walls were solid enough, but the roof always seemed to be complaining, leaking when it rained, baking them when it didn't.

They paid a man named **Reshef** every month for the right to live there. Reshef lived in a much bigger house further inside the city walls. Nadan had never been inside it, but he'd seen the gate: tall, polished, guarded.

We fix it, we worry about it, Nadan thought as he pressed mud into another crack. *But it's not ours.*

That night, lying on his mat, he watched the shadows of raindrops on the ceiling and thought about all the coins that had flowed from his family to Reshef over the years.

Where would we be, he wondered, *if those coins had gone into something we owned instead?*

The next time Arkad spoke in the courtyard, the air was clear and bright again. The storm had washed away the dust, and the city looked newly carved.

The crowd was as large as ever.

"Today," Arkad said, "we will speak of something that is not coins."

The crowd shifted. People had gotten used to his money talk. A change in topic made them nervous and curious at the same time.

"We have spoken of keeping a piece of all you earn," Arkad continued. "We have spoken of making those coins grow and guarding them from foolish loss. Now I ask you:

Where do you lay your head at night?"

People called out:

"In rented rooms!"
  "In my brother's house!"
  "In a corner of my shop!"
  "In my own home," said one proud voice.

Arkad nodded. "Some pay others every month to live in their houses. Some stay with relatives and hope they will never be asked to leave. A few live in homes they themselves own."

He folded his hands.

"When I was young," he said, "I rented a small room. It was crowded, noisy, and expensive. Every month, a part of my hard-earned coins went to my landlord. His house grew stronger. His future grew safer. Mine did not."

He looked around.

"It is not wrong to rent," he said. "Sometimes that is the only choice. But if all your life you pay for a roof that never becomes yours, you are building walls around someone else's future, not your own."

Nadan felt those words land with a weight that felt uncomfortably familiar.

"In time," Arkad went on, "I began to ask myself a question: *What if my monthly payment could slowly turn into ownership instead of disappearing?*"

He smiled slightly.

"So I did what many are afraid to do. I took a long view. I found a small, simple house on the edge of Babylon, one that needed repairs but had solid walls. I made an agreement: I would pay for it a little bit each month, like rent, and as I did, more and more of it would belong to me."

"Wasn't that more expensive?" someone called.

"In the beginning, yes," Arkad said. "I had to be strict with my other spending. Less feasting, fewer luxuries. But as the years passed, a strange thing happened."

He lifted his hand.

"The house stopped being a cost and started being a **strength**."

"It sheltered my family. I no longer feared that a landlord would push us out or raise the price. Part of the land around it grew a garden that fed us. And when Babylon changed and grew, that little house became more and more valuable."

He looked around the courtyard, letting people picture it.

"A dwelling," he said, "is not always just a place to sleep. With planning, it can be a place that protects you, feeds you, and sometimes even earns for you."

He looked toward the group of teenagers without realising how closely they were listening.

"You are young," he said. "You may not be ready to buy a house yet. But you can watch how your families live. You can notice whether all the money flows outward forever, or whether some of it is slowly, quietly building something that will still be there when the rent-collectors are gone."

He leaned back.

"Make of your dwelling, when the time comes, not just a cost, but part of your wealth."

The words hung in the still air.

Nadan thought about his house, the leaking roof, his mother's tired hands.

Not even ours.

As the crowd began to shuffle and drift into side conversations, he felt a new question forming inside him:

If I can't buy a house now, what can I do?

Is there any way, even at my age, to start building something that's ours, not just borrowed?

Later, under the palm tree, they unpacked Arkad's lesson the way they always did.

"So now we need to buy houses," Bela said. "Let me just check my 'small teenage mansion' fund."

Karim laughed. "I think I left mine in my other tunic."

Daria shook her head. "He didn't tell us to run into the market and buy whatever has a roof. He said: 'when the time comes.' But he also said something else." She tapped her clay tablet.

"What?" Nadan asked.

"That paying rent forever means the house owner gets stronger and you stay in the same place," Daria said. "We already know this from our own families. My parents talk about rent all the time."

Bela lay back, staring at the sky through the leaves. "I get the idea," he said. "Owning is better than renting. But we're kids. We barely earn enough for sandals and honey cakes."

"Speak for yourself," Daria said. "I earn enough for scrolls *and* sandals."

Karim looked thoughtful. "Even if we can't buy a house now," he said, "maybe we can start thinking differently about where we live. Like... use it better?"

"What do you mean?" Nadan asked.

Karim shrugged. "I don't know. My uncle runs a little shop out of the front room of his house. He says the house helps pay for itself. That's sort of what Arkad meant, right? A home that 'does something', not just a place to sleep."

Bela perked up. "A house that helps pay for itself," he repeated. "I like that."

Nadan said nothing.

He was thinking about his mother selling small loaves of bread from their doorway sometimes, to neighbours. She already did it quietly, when she had extra flour and energy. It didn't happen often, but when it did, the little coins helped.

We already do a tiny version, he realised. *We just never think of it as the house working for us.*

"Maybe," Nadan said slowly, "we can't buy houses yet. But maybe we can start... using our homes like tiny businesses. A little, anyway. Learning how it works so when we're older, we're not surprised by it."

Daria nodded. "Yes," she said. "Arkad keeps teaching us to think like owners, not just workers. Owners save. Owners invest. Owners think about their home as part of their plan, not just something they pay for."

Bela groaned. "So many plans. So few coins."

Karim grinned. "You were the one wanting to bet all your coins on stormy ships."

"Fair," Bela admitted.

They sat in silence for a bit, listening to the leaves.

Finally Daria said, "Let's do what we always do: turn the lesson into questions for ourselves."

She scratched in the clay:

- How does my family's home take our money?
- Is there any way, now, to make it give some value back?
- What skills would we need, so one day we can turn a home into an advantage instead of a drain?

Bela read it over her shoulder. "And question four," he added, "how do we stop imagining castles and start with something we actually can do?"

They all laughed, but it was a good question.

FIRST COINS

The answer, at least for Nadan, came from his mother's bread.

The next week, he noticed a pattern he'd always ignored. On days when his mother baked bread for their own meals, there was often a little spare dough. Sometimes she shaped it into a few extra small loaves and placed them near the door.

Those days, neighbours would knock.

"Smells good," they'd say shyly. "Do you have one to spare?"

If his mother was tired, she would just give them away. If a little behind on rent, she would ask for a coin.

Nadan watched the coins appear and disappear without anyone calling it a business. It was just "help" or "extra."

"What if it was more than extra?" he wondered aloud one evening, as his mother kneaded dough.

"What do you mean?" she asked.

He wiped the flour off his fingers. "What if, once or twice a week, we baked a little more on purpose. And sold some on purpose. Not just when there's leftover dough. The house always smells good when you bake. People like it. They buy."

His mother paused, hands buried in the dough.

"It's work, Nadan," she said. "Extra wood, extra flour. If no one buys, we waste."

"I know," he said. "But we could test it. Small. Like we did with the shield-maker. We could use a little from our First Coins to buy extra flour for one baking day. If we sell, we put the coins back and keep some as profit. If we don't sell, we eat bread for two days and never do it again."

She looked at him with new eyes.

"You've been listening to Arkad," she said.

He smiled. "Maybe."

She hesitated, then nodded. "We can test," she said. "One day. No more. I will not turn our whole life into a risk."

"Deal," Nadan said.

On the chosen day, their small house turned into a tiny bakery.

His mother woke early and mixed more dough than usual. The whole room filled with the warm smell of yeast and baking bread. Nadan made a simple sign to hang by the door: **FRESH LOAVES – 1 COIN**.

"We don't even have a fancy shop," he said nervously. "What if no one comes?"

"Then we have a lot of bread," his mother said. "And your brothers will be very happy."

But someone did come.

First it was their neighbour, Leila, who bought two loaves because she "hated kneading." Then it was a man who passed by, sniffed the air, and said, "My wife is sick. This will cheer her." He bought one.

By midday, half the loaves were gone.

By evening, they were all gone.

Nadan and his mother counted the coins at the small table, lit by a single lamp.

They did the maths carefully.

Wood cost a little. Flour cost more. But even after subtracting that, they had **extra coins** on the table that would not have existed otherwise.

His mother pushed two of them toward Nadan.

"For your First Coins," she said. "Your idea, your share."

He pushed them back. "We used some of my First Coins to buy the flour," he said. "So these coins are 'their children.' They should go to the First Coins jar. Otherwise, what's the point?"

His mother stared at him, then laughed.

"You're turning into a little Arkad," she said. "Fine. These go to your savings. The rest we'll split, some for the house, some for food."

She folded a few coins away separately.

"Do you see?" she said softly. "The house helped today. I stood in *our* doorway, baked in *our* oven, and the neighbourhood brought coins instead of taking them."

Nadan smiled slowly. "We didn't just pay to live here today," he said. "We got paid, a little, for living here."

He went to bed that night feeling something new: his home might be small, and not even truly theirs yet, but it had just acted like a tiny, tiny version of what Arkad described, a dwelling that wasn't just a cost, but also a source of value.

At the palm tree, the others had their own stories.

"My father laughed at Arkad's 'home lesson' at first," Karim said. "But then he stopped and started counting on his fingers. He realised we've been paying rent to the same man for years. He said, 'I think I've bought that house twice over. I just don't own any of it.' He's now saving to try to buy a small place further out, even if it's rough at first."

"That's a big goal," Daria said. "It will take years."

"Yes," Karim said. "He knows. But he also said: 'Years are going to pass anyway. I may as well aim them at something.'"

Bela scratched his neck. "My parents aren't thinking about houses at all," he said. "But my mother does sew cloaks. She started hanging a few outside the door so passers-by can see.

Last week someone bought one. She got excited. Now I think half our home is going to turn into a cloak factory."

They laughed.

Daria shrugged. "My family already owns our house," she said. "My grandfather bought it long ago. But hearing Arkad made my father realise something: the house has a roof space we never use. He wants to build a small extra room to rent out to a travelling merchant. Says that way, the house helps pay for our food."

"Look at us," Bela said. "The 'Empty Pockets' club planning extended real-estate strategies."

Nadan grinned. "We're still just starting," he said. "But we're thinking like this: not just 'how do we survive this week,' but 'what can we build that will still be here later.'"

Daria put down her clay tablet with a little slap.

"Arkad's point isn't that everyone must own a big fancy house," she said. "It's that if all your payments go outward forever, you will always feel like the ground can disappear under your feet. But if at least some of your effort is slowly building something solid, your savings, your skills, your home, then each year, life gets a little less fragile."

Karim snapped his fingers. "That's it," he said. "Less fragile."

They sat quietly for a moment, each thinking about what "less fragile" might look like in their own lives.

For Nadan, it looked like a roof that didn't leak, a landlord who couldn't throw them out, a room where his mother's bread smells drew customers instead of just feeding whoever happened to pass by.

For Bela, it looked like parents who didn't have to borrow from relatives every month.

For Daria, it looked like choices. A future where she could say yes or no to offers because she wasn't desperate.

That evening, as the sun turned the city gold again, Nadan passed Reshef's big house—the landlord's house.

He looked at the polished gate, the sturdy walls, the high roof that probably never leaked. He thought of the coins his family had paid over the years, joining coins from many other families, all being turned into this one man's security.

He played the long game, Nadan realised. *He turned other people's rent into his own home.*

The thought didn't make him angry. It made him determined.

I won't feel guilty about not being there yet, he told himself. *But I won't walk through life blind to where my coins are going, either.*

He placed his hand on the pouch at his belt.

Inside were his First Coins, some of which now had "children" from the shield-maker and the bread test. They weren't enough to buy a house. Not even close.

But they were the start of something that could.

One day, he thought. *When it's my turn, I'll make my dwelling part of my strength, not just a monthly worry.*

He walked home, the sky turning dark, the city lights flickering on one by one.

Babylon hadn't changed much since the day he'd joined the Empty Pockets Club.

But Nadan had.

He was slowly collecting something invisible but powerful: **a set of ideas about money, work, and home that would guide every choice he made from now on.**

6

Future You

The day started with a broken cart.

Nadan was running an errand for the scribe when he heard a sharp crack and a shout. In the middle of the street, a delivery cart's axle snapped. The front half dropped, jars rolled everywhere, and the driver's scream cut through the noise.

His leg was pinned under the side of the cart.

People rushed over, lifting, pulling, shouting orders. Nadan helped drag the man clear. The leg didn't look right. It bent where it shouldn't.

"Don't move him," someone said. "Get the healer."

The driver's face was pale with shock and pain. Between clenched teeth, he kept saying the same thing over and over:

"I can't miss work. I can't miss work. I can't miss work."

Nadan understood. If the man couldn't pull a cart, he couldn't earn. If he couldn't earn, the rent collectors and moneylenders wouldn't care that his leg was broken.

What happens to someone like him, Nadan thought, *when he just... can't work?*

The question followed him all day.

That afternoon, Arkad spoke again in the courtyard.

Nadan, Bela, Daria, and Karim made sure to arrive early. The story of the broken cart spilled out of Nadan as soon as they met.

"That's awful," Karim said. "Will the cart owner at least help him?"

"Maybe," Nadan said. "Maybe not. But what scared me was how terrified he was of missing work. Like the world would end."

"In a way, it does," Daria said quietly. "If all your money comes from your body working, and your body stops, then... yes. It feels like the world ends."

Bela looked uncomfortable. "I don't like this topic," he said. "Can we go back to bread and shields?"

But when Arkad began speaking, it turned out he *was* going to talk about exactly that topic.

Not broken carts specifically.

Something bigger.

"Today," Arkad said, once the courtyard had settled, "we will talk about **future you**."

He let the phrase hang there for a moment.

"When I was young," he continued, "I thought only about the present. How to survive this month. How to enjoy this evening. How to pay this bill. Over time, I learned to think about next year. And then I forced myself to think about a much older man."

He touched his own chest.

"The man I am now," he said. "Old, slower. Not able to write tablets all day. Not able to run around the city chasing work."

He smiled faintly.

"When I was young, I did not care about him," he said. "But he cared very much about me. He was watching from the future, hoping I would not be foolish."

A few people chuckled.

Arkad leaned forward.

"If you are wise, you do not wait until you are old to worry about being old. You start building a safety net while you are young and strong."

He pointed at the crowd.

"Look around," he said. "Babylon is full of people who, in their youth, said, 'I will always be strong. I will always be able to work.' Now they are bent, tired, sick. Some of them beg. Some must depend entirely on children who can barely support themselves."

Nadan thought of old men he'd seen near the gates, leaning on staffs, hands outstretched for coins.

"I am not mocking them," Arkad said softly. "I am warning you. Illness, accidents, age, they come for all of us. You cannot control *that*. But you can control whether you arrive at that time with nothing, or with something that keeps feeding you even when your body is tired."

He let the silence stretch.

A woman near the front raised her hand. "What if we don't have extra?" she asked. "We already save one coin in ten. We already try to invest. How can we also think about being old?"

Arkad nodded. "That is exactly when you must think about it," he said. "Because the same actions that grow your wealth now can protect you later, if you give some of them a clear **purpose**."

He held up three fingers.

"There are three ways to care for future you:

1. Build savings and investments that you do not plan to touch for a long time.
2. Create sources of income that can continue even when you are not working much.
3. Protect the people who depend on you so they are not destroyed if something happens to you."

Bela muttered, "That's a lot of responsibility."

Daria elbowed him. "You wanted to be rich," she whispered. "This is the real price."

Arkad continued.

"In my middle years," he said, "when my trade was strong and my income was good, I made a rule: a part of my profits would be put aside, never to be used for feasts or clothes or even new business ventures. That part was for old Arkad only."

He smiled.

"Today, that old man thanks the younger one," he said.

The crowd chuckled.

"Some of those coins went into land that would be rented out. Some went into trusted businesses that sent me a share of their profits. Some stayed as simple stored value, so that if the world shook, I would not be completely broken."

He looked around the courtyard.

"You are not all traders," he said. "Some of you are farmers, bakers, scribes, builders. But the rule is the same: decide that **a part** of what you build will be kept for the time when you cannot build as much."

He paused.

"If you begin when you are young, even a small part will grow large over many years. If you wait until your hair turns grey, it is much harder."

Nadan felt a strange mix of fear and relief. Fear, because he saw how fragile many people's lives were. Relief, because Arkad was saying: *You can start now. You don't have to wait until it's too late.*

"What about people who have families?" a man asked. "Who must support children and a wife? How can they think about this future man too?"

Arkad's eyes softened.

"That is when it matters even more," he said. "Because if something happens to you, an accident, sickness, what will they live on? This is why I say: treat part of your wealth as if it does not exist for daily spending. It belongs to your old age and to those who depend on you."

He nodded once, firmly.

"Forget this rule," he said, "and your future self may curse your name. Keep it, and he will bless you."

The way he said it made the hair on Nadan's arms stand up.

As the talk ended and the crowd began to move, Nadan wasn't sure whether he felt older or younger.

He just knew that somewhere out there, the "old Nadan" he would one day become was watching and hoping he didn't mess this up.

Under the palm tree, the mood was more serious than usual.

"No offence," Bela said, "but I did not sign up to think this far ahead. I barely know what I'm eating tomorrow."

Karim stared at the ground. "I keep thinking about the cart driver," he said. "What if that was my father? Or me, in ten years?"

Daria balanced her clay tablet on her knees. "We've been learning how to treat our money better," she said. "Now we also have to treat our **time** better. It's not just 'now' time. It's 'later' time too."

Nadan scratched patterns in the dust.

"When Arkad talks about 'future you,'" he said slowly, "I picture an older version of myself sitting somewhere, watching me. He doesn't get a say. He just lives with whatever I decide. That feels… unfair."

Bela shuddered. "Stop. That image is horrible. Old me is definitely judging my snack choices."

Karim smiled weakly. "Mine is judging my procrastination."

Daria tapped her stylus thoughtfully. "I think the point is simple," she said. "Some of our coins should be for **today,** food, shelter, small joys. Some should be for **growth,** investments, learning. And some should be for **future us,** set aside to protect us when we can't do as much."

She drew three circles in the clay and labelled them: **Now**, **Growing**, **Future**.

"We already have 'Now' and 'Growing,'" she said. "We save and invest. But we've never said, 'This part is for when I'm old. I will not touch it before then, unless there is truly no choice.'"

"That sounds strict," Bela said.

"It is," Daria replied. "But not as strict as begging in your seventies."

Karim winced. "Fair."

They sat quietly for a bit.

Finally Nadan said, "What would this look like *for us*, right now? We're not going to buy land tomorrow. We don't have wives and children yet. How do teenagers 'take care of future them'?"

They thought about it.

"I have an idea," Daria said at last. "We already save one coin in ten. And from that, we put some into investments. What if we decide that a slice of our savings, like, say, one coin out of every **twenty** we earn, is specifically for future us?"

"Meaning?" Karim asked.

"Meaning we do not plan to spend it until we're much older," Daria said. "We still invest it wisely, so it grows. But we don't use it to upgrade houses, buy nicer clothes, start risky ventures. It's *there* for bad years, illness, old age."

Bela made a face. "So we add another rule: 'Some money is locked away for Grey-Hair Bela'?"

"Yes," Daria said. "Exactly that."

Bela thought about it. "Grey-Hair Bela sounds annoying," he

said. "But I'd rather he be annoying and safe than miserable and blaming me."

Karim nodded slowly. "I like it," he said. "Even if we start with a tiny amount, it's something. It's... respect for our future life."

Nadan pictured a little pile of coins sitting by a door marked "Do not open until future." It was both scary and strangely comforting.

"I'm in," he said. "One in twenty, for Future Nadan. We still have plenty for Now and Growing."

Daria wrote it down:

Future You Rule:
From everything we earn, at least 1 coin in 20 is for our older selves. We still invest it, but we do not spend it on present wants.

The next few weeks changed the way they saw almost everything.

When they earned from jobs, they automatically divided their coins into:

- **Now** (daily life)
- **Growing** (investments and business tests like the bread)
- **Future** (the "untouchable" stash)

It wasn't perfect. Sometimes reality punched through.

One week, Karim's little brother got sick, and his family had to spend more than expected on medicine and care. Karim took some of his "Future You" coins and used them to help.

He felt guilty.

When he confessed under the palm tree, Daria shook her head.

"That's exactly what it's *for*," she said. "It's not a prison. It's a shield. Family sickness is not an excuse, it's the reason we're doing this. You used it wisely."

Nadan nodded. "The rule isn't 'never touch,'" he said. "It's 'don't touch it lightly.' Spend it when **life** demands it, not when snacks demand it."

Bela clutched his chest. "My snacks are part of life," he protested.

"Future You disagrees," Daria said.

They laughed, but the underlying idea stuck:

Future money is not magic. It's just normal money we decide to respect more.

One evening, Nadan's mother noticed something.

"You've been quieter lately," she said as they cleaned up after dinner. "But not in a sad way. In a... calculating way." She narrowed her eyes playfully. "What are you planning, exactly?"

Nadan hesitated. Then he told her about Arkad's talk, about thinking of "future Nadan," about the three circles.

His mother listened, washing bowls, hands moving automatically.

"You sound like your grandfather," she said at last. "He used to say, 'When you are young, you carry money. When you are old, you want money to carry you.'"

"What happened to him?" Nadan asked.

"He never got to build much," she said softly. "War took a lot. But the little he did build is the reason I was able to survive after he died. He had a few hidden coins, some stored grain, a small piece of land. Without that, I might never have reached Babylon."

She looked at him seriously.

"You are doing a good thing," she said. "Not just for yourself, but for whatever family you may have one day. Imagine if your children see their father calm when trouble comes, because he prepared."

Nadan swallowed, suddenly overwhelmed.

"I'm still just... me," he said. "I'm not a father, I'm not old, I'm not rich."

"Exactly," his mother said. "That's when you start."

She wiped her hands and touched his cheek gently.

"Future you is lucky," she said. "He has you."

A few days later, they saw the cart driver again.

He was sitting on a low bench outside a small house, a crutch leaning against the wall. His leg was wrapped in cloth, and he was using a carved stick to roll small stones back and forth, clearly bored out of his mind.

Nadan went over.

"How's your leg?" he asked.

The man shrugged. "Healing, they say. I'll walk again. Maybe even pull a cart someday. But not soon."

"Who's paying you while you heal?" Bela asked bluntly.

"Paying me?" The man laughed without humour. "No one pays a broken cart driver. My brothers help. A kind neighbour brought bread. The landlord still wants his money."

Karim looked pained. "Don't you have... any savings?"

"Some," the man said. "I used them already. They leaked away faster than blood from a cut."

He squinted up at the sky.

"If I'd saved more when I could walk," he muttered, "I'd be less scared sitting here. Maybe next time I will. If there is a next time."

They walked away quietly.

No one made jokes this time.

"So that's what it looks like," Karim said. "No Future You planning."

Bela nodded. "Or Future You planning that started too late."

Daria squeezed her clay tablet.

"We are not better than him," she said firmly. "We're just hearing these lessons earlier. That means we have less excuse."

They all nodded.

The weight of that responsibility pressed down on them, not in a crushing way, but like a hand on their shoulders steering them gently forward.

That evening under the palm tree, they summarised the new lesson.

Daria wrote:

Lessons about Future You:

- One day, you will be older, weaker, or unable to work as hard. That is guaranteed.
- You can start helping that future version of you now, with even small amounts.
- Treat some of your money as "not for now." Respect it. Don't use it for small desires.
- Use it when life really hits, or when you are old and work less. Not before.

Bela added one more, half-joking, half-serious:

- Future You is a real person. Try not to make him hate you.

They laughed.

But Nadan, staring at the sunset over Babylon's walls, imagined an older man with his eyes, sitting calmly while storms raged outside, because younger Nadan had made a few simple, boring, wise decisions.

He won't have everything, Nadan thought. *But he won't have nothing.*

That felt like a victory worth working for.

7

Levelling Up Your Skills

A week later, Nadan noticed something strange.

He was copying a long legal tablet for a merchant, names, dates, numbers, all cramped together. A year ago, this kind of job would have drained his brain dry. He'd have finished exhausted, with ink stains on his hands and a headache behind his eyes.

Today, he finished faster.

His writing was cleaner. He spotted a mistake in the original text and quietly corrected it. When he handed the tablet back, his master, the scribe, frowned, not with anger, but with surprise.

"You're getting good," the man said. "Very good."

It was a simple sentence, but it stuck in Nadan's chest like a shiny pin.

I'm getting good.

He walked home thinking about it.

They'd learned how to **save**.
 They'd learned how to **invest**.
 They'd learned how to **protect** their money and think about **future them**.

But all of that was built on one thing:

The coins they earned in the first place.

What if that part could grow too?

Arkad's next talk in the courtyard was shorter than usual, but it might have been the most important.

"Today," he said, "we will talk about something that looks simple but changes everything:

Your ability to earn."

He paced slowly in front of them.

"Imagine two men," he said. "Both save one coin in ten. Both invest wisely. But one earns ten coins a month, and the other earns a hundred. Over time, who will grow wealth faster?"

"The second," someone called.

"Of course," Arkad said. "The rules are the same for both. But the one who can bring more coins into his life has more to save, more to invest, more to build with."

He looked around.

"So ask yourself this question, and ask it often:

How can I become more valuable?
   Not 'How can I get rich quickly?'
   Not 'How can I trick someone into paying me more?'
   How can I become the kind of person whose work is worth more to others?"

He let that sink in.

"When I was a young scribe," Arkad continued, "I was clumsy. Slow. My writing was messy. I earned little. Then I watched the best scribes, how they held their stylus, how they arranged their work, how they checked for mistakes. I copied them. I practised at night. I asked questions."

He smiled.

"In time, people started asking for me by name. They trusted my tablets. Merchants said, 'If Arkad wrote it, it must be correct.' My master needed me more. My pay grew."

He lifted a finger.

"Your job is not just 'what you do.' It is a skill you can sharpen. A tool you can upgrade. If you sharpen it, you will earn more. If you let it rust, you will always be cheap."

The crowd murmured.

A young man called out, "But what if my job is boring? I just carry baskets in the market."

"Then become the best basket carrier in Babylon," Arkad said without missing a beat. "Strong, reliable, on time, honest. People pay more for those they trust."

He pointed at another man. "If you are a cook, learn new dishes. If you are a builder, learn to read plans, not just lift stones. If you are a trader, learn numbers and reading so you can understand contracts. If you are a scribe…" He smiled toward Nadan's area, though he might not have meant him specifically. "…learn the language of business, law, and numbers, not just letters."

He spread his hands.

"Never say, 'This is all I can do.' Say instead, 'This is what I can do **today**. What can I add to it?'"

He paused, then added one more line:

"Your mind is your greatest asset. If you feed it, it will feed you."

And with that, he ended the talk.

It was so short that people blinked, wondering if there would be more. There wasn't.

Just that one idea: **become more valuable.**

Under the palm tree, they didn't joke at first.

"I don't like this chapter," Bela said eventually. "The others were about money. This one is about... me. That's harder."

Karim nodded. "It's easier to say, 'I'll save a coin,' than to say, 'I'll become better.'"

Daria uncovered the clay tablet.

"That's exactly why it matters," she said. "We can't control everything out there, markets, weather, traders, landlords. But we can control what we know, how we work, and how useful we are."

She looked at each of them.

"So," she asked, "what could *you* do to become more valuable in the next year?"

They went quiet.

Karim spoke first.

"I help my uncle sometimes," he said. "He builds furniture. Right now I just carry wood and sweep. But I like the actual building. If I learned properly, I could become more than a helper. People always need good furniture. Tables, beds, doors…"

"That's a skill that travels," Daria said. "Wood is everywhere. So are people with backs and homes."

Karim smiled a little. "Maybe I'll ask my uncle to teach me. Not just 'move this,' but 'show me how.' Even if he doesn't pay more at first, I'll learn more. That's worth something."

Daria nodded approvingly.

"What about you, Bela?" she asked.

He groaned. "Do we have to?"

"Yes," all three replied.

Bela stared at the dirt. "I… I'm good with people," he said slowly. "Talking. Convincing. I got you all to at least consider the purple-cloth disaster."

"That's not a selling point," Daria muttered.

"Still," Nadan said, "it's true. You can talk to anyone. Strangers like you."

Bela shrugged, but he didn't disagree.

"My father sells goods in the market," he admitted. "Sometimes he lets me talk to customers. I notice when I'm there, he sells more. Not always because I'm clever. Sometimes just because I'm louder."

They laughed.

"But I don't know how to turn that into something... real," Bela said. "Like a proper skill, not just being annoying."

"Sales is a skill," Daria said firmly. "Persuasion, reading people, handling numbers, not lying. You could learn how the best traders keep records, manage regular customers, arrange deals. If you become *known* as someone who can bring in business, that's value."

Bela looked thoughtful for a change. "So instead of just helping sometimes," he said, "I could ask my father to really teach me. Let me handle a small stall for a few hours. Track what I sell. Prove I can increase his profit."

"Exactly," Daria said. "Then, whether you work with him or someone else later, you're not just 'another boy in the market.' You're 'the one who brings in customers.'"

Bela's eyes lit up a little. "I... kind of like that."

Daria turned to Nadan.

"And you?" she asked. "You're already a scribe."

LEVELLING UP YOUR SKILLS

Nadan thought of his master's words that morning. *You're getting good.*

"I copy tablets," he said. "But I'm starting to see how the numbers and contracts actually work. The merchant whose tablet I copied today, he talked to my master about interest, profits, partnerships. I understood almost everything."

Daria raised her eyebrows. "That's not nothing."

"What if I learn more about that?" Nadan said, warming to the idea. "Not just writing the words, but understanding the deals. Maybe one day I can write contracts that protect people from bad terms. Or help them plan loans wisely. Or advise them. People pay for advice that saves them from mistakes."

"Little Arkad," Bela said fondly.

Nadan smiled. "I'm not Arkad. But he did say his teacher explained money to him. Maybe I can learn enough to explain it to others who can't just walk into Arkad's courtyard."

Daria looked pleased. "That's real value," she said. "Clear thinking. Clear writing. Helping others avoid traps."

She covered her tablet and looked at all three boys.

"I'm lucky," she said. "My father already trusts me with some of the family accounts. I can already read and write, and I like numbers. If I get really good at keeping records, planning spending and saving, maybe one day I can run accounts for merchants. Or teach other families how to plan their coins. Or run my own business properly without drowning in confusion."

"And you'll yell at us for our bad maths," Bela added.

"Absolutely," Daria said.

The next few weeks, they didn't just talk about "skills."

They changed how they spent their **time**.

Karim stayed late at his uncle's workshop instead of running off after sweeping.

"Show me how you measure for a table," he asked. "Why this wood, not that one? How do you price it?"

At first, his uncle waved him away. Then, seeing he was serious, he started handing Karim small tasks: sanding edges, checking angles, eventually helping assemble simple stools.

His muscles hurt more. But his mind buzzed.

Bela, for once, got serious in the market.

"Let me run this side of the stall for the morning," he told his father. "If I sell less than you, I'll shut up. If I sell more, you teach me properly."

His father laughed, but agreed.

By noon, Bela had sold more, mostly by calling out to passers-by with smart jokes and throwing in tiny extras that cost them almost nothing but made customers smile.

His father scratched his head.

"You might be good at this," he said. "Annoyingly good."

"Then teach me to be better," Bela said.

So his father did.

He showed him how to track repeat customers, how to order just enough stock, how to offer credit to the right people and *not* to the wrong ones. Bela wrote down things he'd never noticed before.

Nadan asked his master if he could help check numbers, not just letters.

"At the end of the day," he said, "when you balance your accounts, can I watch? Maybe help?"

His master looked at him cautiously, then agreed.

Nadan learned how to see patterns in income and spending, how to spot missing coins, how to structure tablets so merchants understood them quickly. He stayed late a few evenings, tired but excited.

Daria doubled down on everything.

She asked her father if she could take over one small part of the household budget, oil and grain costs, for three months.

"I'll track prices," she said. "Find the best times and places to buy. See if I can save us something *without* lowering how much we eat."

Her father raised an eyebrow, amused and impressed. "If you can do that," he said, "I'll let you handle more."

So she did.

She created simple charts on clay, watched prices in different markets, quietly changed where and when they bought from. At the end of three months, she showed her father how much they'd saved.

It wasn't huge.

But it was real.

And it repeated every month.

Her father stared at the numbers.

"I knew you were smart," he said. "I didn't realise your work could make this much difference."

Under the palm tree, everything felt different.

They were still the same four teenagers. Same sandals, same

city, same problems.

But their **trajectory** was changing.

"I'm still not earning more *yet*," Karim said. "But my uncle is letting me help with more advanced tasks. He says, 'Once you can build a whole table yourself, I can trust you with more money work.'"

"Same," Nadan said. "My pay hasn't gone up, but my master is giving me more important tablets. Merchant contracts, not just shopping lists. That's a sign."

Bela grinned. "My father already promised me a bigger share of profit if I keep bringing in customers," he said. "He said, 'Talk less nonsense, more business,' which is *harsh* but fair."

Daria smiled. "Even if the coins don't show up immediately," she said, "we're doing something important: we're making ourselves harder to replace."

She wrote on the clay tablet:

"Increasing Your Ability to Earn" means:

- Learning more about your current work so you become better at it.
- Adding new skills that fit with what you already do.
- Becoming known as someone who is reliable, honest, and useful.
- Using your mind, not just your hands.

"Arkad's right," she added. "Your mind really *is* your greatest asset. No one can steal it. No landlord can raise the rent on it. No storm can sink it."

Bela tilted his head. "Storms can hit it," he said. "Especially if it's mine."

They laughed.

But beneath the jokes, something solid was forming.

They weren't just saving coins anymore.

They were upgrading **the source** of those coins.

That night, walking home through streets lit by small lamps, Nadan felt strangely powerful.

Not because he was rich—he wasn't.
 Not because he knew everything—he didn't.

But because, for the first time, he saw a clear path:

- Learn more.
- Become better at real things people need.
- Use that to earn more.
- Use **that** to save, invest, protect, and plan.

It all joined together like pieces of a puzzle:

1. **Save a part of all you earn.**
2. **Control your spending.**
3. **Make your money grow.**
4. **Guard it from bad deals.**
5. **Use your home wisely.**
6. **Plan for Future You.**
7. **Keep improving your skills so all of the above gets bigger over time.**

This is the real game, he thought. *Not just chasing coins, but becoming someone who knows what to do with them, and someone people want to pay.*

He smiled to himself as he turned the corner toward his small, not-yet-owned house, where the smell of his mother's bread drifted into the street.

Future Nadan didn't feel like a stranger anymore.

He felt like a teammate waiting further down the road, cheering him on.

8

Escaping the Debt Trap

Debt had always been part of Babylon.

You could see it in little ways: a neighbour whispering with a moneylender in a corner, a shopkeeper's smile freezing when a "customer" came in who only ever promised to pay later, the way people walked faster when they saw a creditor approaching.

But for Nadan and his friends, debt had mostly been background noise.

Until it crashed into their lives through someone they knew.

His name was **Rafi**.

He was a few years older than them, quick with a joke and quicker with his hands. He did odd jobs, carrying loads, helping in shops, messenger work. Rafi always seemed busy, always seemed to be chasing something.

He also always seemed to be just a little behind.

One evening, the First Coins group found him sitting alone near the city wall, head in his hands.

"Rafi?" Nadan asked. "You okay?"

Rafi looked up. His eyes were red.

"I'm fine," he said automatically. Then he laughed, a strange, sharp sound. "No, I'm not. I'm smashed."

Bela dropped down beside him. "What happened?" he asked.

Rafi hesitated. Then the words spilled out.

"I owe money," he said. "Too much. First I borrowed a little to buy better tools. Then to fix a mistake I made. Then to pay rent one month when work was bad. Then to pay back the first lender. It kept… rolling."

He clenched his fists.

"Every time I thought I was almost clear," he said, "someone else wanted their share. One lender charges me for every month I'm late. Another wants a piece of every job I do. Now they're all shouting at once."

Karim swallowed. "How much do you owe?"

Rafi told them.

It was a terrifying number for someone with no steady job and no plan.

"I can't breathe," Rafi said. "I get up in the morning and every coin already belongs to someone else. I'm tired before I even start."

Daria's face hardened.

"Who lent you this money?" she asked. "Are they honest men or sharks?"

"Both," Rafi said bitterly. "Some helped me when I really needed it. Others just saw an opportunity. But it doesn't matter. I said yes. I signed their tablets. The law is on their side."

He pushed his hands through his hair.

"One of them said if I don't pay something this month, he'll take my tools," he said. "Another threatened to talk to the city guards. I can't see a way out."

Bela looked shaken. "Can't you... borrow from someone else to pay them back?"

Rafi stared at him.

"That's what I've been doing," he said quietly. "That's **exactly** how I got here."

Silence.

The four friends had been learning how to grow and guard coins. But debt was the opposite: **coins flowing backward**, pulled by promises from the past.

"We have to help him," Karim said. "We can't just walk away."

"With what?" Rafi asked. "Your club savings? A few coins won't fix this. They'll just disappear into the hole."

He stood up abruptly.

"Forget it," he said. "I shouldn't have dumped this on you."

He walked away before they could answer.

Bela kicked at the dirt. "I hate this," he said. "He's right. If we give him our savings, it'll vanish. But if we do nothing, we're just… watching him drown."

"Then we need a better plan," Daria said. "Not patching a hole with a leaf. Something real."

"Like what?" Karim asked.

Daria bit her lip. "I don't know yet," she said. "Maybe Arkad does."

The answer came from higher up than they expected.

A few days later, the whole city buzzed with news: **the king himself** had spoken about debt.

Rumours flew.

"Too many people are slaves to their lenders," one man said.
  "The king is worried they can't fight if enemies attack," said another.
  "I heard he asked Arkad for advice," a woman whispered.

At first, it sounded like just another story. Babylon always had stories about the king.

Then, one afternoon, proclamations were read aloud in the marketplace.

A royal crier climbed onto a platform, uncovered a long tablet, and shouted:

"By order of the king of Babylon!
  Those drowning in debt may seek help in a new plan to repay what they owe **without becoming slaves forever**.
  The plan was designed with the counsel of Arkad, the richest man in Babylon.
  Those who come must be ready to work, save, and follow rules.
  This is not a gift. It is a path."

The words hit Nadan like a lightning bolt.

"Arkad," he breathed.

Bela grabbed his arm. "This is it," he said. "This is for Rafi."

Karim nodded. "If the king is involved," he said, "the lenders will have to listen."

Daria's eyes were already on the clay tablet in her hand.

"I want to know exactly how this 'plan' works," she said. "If it comes from Arkad, it will be clear. Maybe we can copy it."

The next day, they found themselves in a new kind of gathering.

Not Arkad's courtyard this time, but a large public hall near one of the city's main gates. People who owed money sat on one side, worried, tense, hopeful. On the other side sat lenders, some annoyed, some curious, some stone-faced.

In the middle, by a stone table with a royal seal, stood a scribe reading out the plan.

Nadan felt a strange shiver. *One day, that could be me,* he thought. *Writing plans that change people's lives.*

He forced himself to focus.

The scribe read:

"Those who owe more than they can pay shall not be thrown

into endless slavery, if they agree to the following:

1. They must list **all** their debts honestly.
2. They must commit to paying a steady part of their earnings each month to their creditors.
3. They must agree to live simply until their debts are cleared.
4. They may keep a small share of their earnings to rebuild their own strength, so they do not fall into new debt.
5. Their creditors, in turn, agree to accept steady payments and to stop adding endless new charges, so long as the debtor follows the plan."

The hall murmured.

It was not a free pass. It was not "your debt is cancelled." It was a **structure**.

A path out of the pit.

The scribe continued, now speaking as Arkad might have spoken:

"To escape debt, one must do three things:

- Stop digging deeper.
- Make a clear, honest plan.
- Follow it with discipline until the burden is gone."

Rafi was there.

The four friends found him in the crowd, looking like someone who hadn't slept in days.

"You came," Nadan said.

"I had to try," Rafi said. "If this doesn't work, I don't know what will."

They stayed with him as he went through the process.

A royal clerk sat at the stone table with a stylus.

"Name," the clerk said.

"Rafi bin Oren."

"List your debts," the clerk said.

Rafi swallowed hard and began.

This moneylender. That shopkeeper. The trader who'd lent him silver for tools. The friend he'd promised to pay back "soon" and then avoided in the street.

Seeing it all written down made his face go grey.

The clerk didn't react. He just kept writing.

When Rafi finished, the clerk read back the total and then said,

"Now: how much do you earn in an average month?"

Rafi gave the number, ashamed.

The clerk did some quick calculations.

"You cannot pay this all at once," he said. "But you can pay it over time. Here is Arkad's suggestion, approved by the king."

He spoke slowly, like a teacher:

"From everything you earn each month, you will:

- Keep enough for basic food and shelter. No luxuries.
- Set aside **at least 20%** to repay your debts, split fairly among your creditors.
- Set aside a **small part,** even just one coin in ten of what remains, for yourself, to rebuild. You cannot give away everything and stay strong."

Rafi stared.

"So I still pay myself?" he asked. "Even in debt?"

"Yes," the clerk said. "If you give every coin to your creditors, you will grow weaker and desperate. Desperate men make bad promises and fall into worse traps. A small part is for your future, so you never come back here again."

He looked around the room, making sure others were listening.

"Debt is a weight," he said. "But if you carry it steadily, without adding more, it shrinks. Slowly, but it shrinks."

One by one, Rafi's creditors came to the table.

Each listened as the clerk explained the plan.

"This is what he will pay you," the clerk said. "You may not get it all at once. But you will get something, regularly. And the king expects you to accept this and **stop choking him with new charges**, as long as he keeps his part."

Some lenders grumbled.

One walked away in anger.

Most agreed, even if reluctantly. A royal seal had a way of making stubborn men behave.

At the end, Rafi walked out with a tablet of his own, his **repayment plan,** pressed into his hands.

It contained:

- His total debt.
- A monthly amount he had to pay.
- A promise to himself that he would live simply until it was done.
- A small line: "One coin in ten of what remains after bare

needs shall be kept to rebuild his own strength."

He clutched it like a lifeline.

Under the palm tree, the friends broke it down.

"So now he's not drowning," Karim said. "He's… swimming with a heavy stone, but at least he's moving."

Daria nodded. "Before, he had **no structure**. Just fear and random payments. Now he has a plan."

Bela chewed his lip. "I'm glad the king helped," he said. "But not everyone will have a king to rescue them. What if it was just us?"

"Then we'd copy Arkad," Daria said. "Honest list of debts. Promise to stop borrowing more. Decide a realistic amount to pay every month, and stick to it. Pay some to everyone, so no one is ignored. And still keep a tiny piece for ourselves, so we don't break."

She wrote on the clay tablet:

Debt Escape Rules (Arkad-style):

1. **Face the truth.** List every debt. No hiding, no pretending.
2. **Stop digging.** Take no new debt, except maybe in true life-or-death emergencies.

3. **Make a plan.** Decide what % of your income goes to debt every month (e.g., 20%).
4. **Pay everyone something** regularly, not just the loudest creditor.
5. **Still pay yourself a little**, so you can rebuild and never go back.

"And rule six," Bela added quietly. "Don't be proud. Ask for help early, before it gets this bad."

They all went quiet, thinking of Rafi.

"I want to help him," Karim said. "But not by throwing money into the hole."

"Then help him with work," Daria said. "Introduce him to people who can pay him fairly. Encourage him when he wants to give up. Remind him to follow his plan."

"Be his support, not his sponsor," Nadan added.

They all nodded.

The next few months were hard on Rafi.

He worked long hours, taking every honest job he could. He sold a few things he didn't truly need. He cut out treats, parties, anything that cost extra. Every month, he made his payments like the plan said.

It didn't magically fix his life.

Some days he was angry and short-tempered. Some days he wanted to give up.

But the debt number on his tablet slowly, undeniably, went down.

Occasionally, when he could, he dropped by the palm tree.

"I paid off **this** lender completely," he said once, tapping the tablet with something like pride. "Now my payments go to fewer people. It's still heavy, but... lighter."

"That's how it works," Daria said. "Step by step."

On another day, he showed them a small pouch.

"This is my 'never again' money," he said. "The bit I pay myself like Arkad said. If anything bad happens once I'm free, I'll use this instead of borrowing."

Nadan smiled. "Welcome to the First Coins style," he said.

Rafi laughed weakly. "I wish I'd joined your club before I needed the king," he said.

"Me too," Bela said. "But at least now we know how bad it can get."

One evening, Arkad passed by their usual spot.

They weren't expecting him. He was just walking with a servant, headed somewhere else. But when he saw the familiar cluster of four under the palm tree, and now sometimes Rafi, too, he paused.

"How goes your learning?" he asked.

"Slow and steady," Daria said.

"Like good money," Arkad replied.

Bela couldn't help himself.

"Is there one rule you think is the most important?" he blurted out. "If you had to pick?"

Arkad thought for a moment.

"No," he said. "There is no single rule. They support each other. Saving without learning to earn more is slow. Earning more without self-control is wasteful. Investing without caution is dangerous. Planning without action is fantasy."

He looked at each of them in turn.

"But if I had to choose something," he said, "I would say this: **respect reality**."

They frowned.

"Reality?" Karim asked.

"Yes," Arkad said. "Reality is: coins obey certain patterns. If you always spend more than you earn, reality wins, not your hopes. If you pretend a bad deal is safe because you want it to be, reality wins, not your feelings. If you close your eyes to debt, it still grows."

He tapped his temple.

"Respect what is true, not just what you wish was true. Then build from there. That is what all my 'rules' are really about."

He smiled at them, something like pride in his eyes.

"You have time," he said. "Many here do not. Use it well."

Then he walked on, leaving them under the tree with more to think about than ever.

That night, Nadan lay awake and thought about everything they'd learned:

- **Save first, always.**
- **Control spending.**
- **Invest wisely.**
- **Avoid get-rich-quick traps.**
- **Use your home smartly.**
- **Plan for future you.**
- **Grow your skills.**
- **Face debt honestly and escape it with a plan.**

He imagined these ideas like stones, forming a path across a dangerous river.

On one side: chaos, fear, drowning in debt, always being surprised by trouble.

On the other side: not perfection, not magic riches, but **stability**. Enough. The ability to help others instead of needing rescue.

He wasn't on the far bank yet.

But he had his feet on the stones.

And that, he realised, was the real gift Arkad had given them:

Not money.

A map.

9

What Does "Rich" Even Mean?

The first person to call them "rich" did it as an insult.

It was at the market, on a hot afternoon when the air felt like baked bread. Nadan and Bela were helping Bela's father at the stall. Business had been good, busy, but not crazy.

A boy their age wandered over, hands in his pockets. His name was **Yoram**, and he always seemed to have a group around him, laughing too loudly at his jokes.

He picked up a small carved toy from the stall, turned it over, and smirked.

"So," Yoram said, "I heard you lot are becoming *money experts*."

Bela's shoulders tensed. "We're just working," he said. "Like everyone else."

Yoram snorted. "Sure. Except you've always got coins now. Rafi says you helped him with some 'Arkad plan.' Daria's father says she's saving like a banker. Even Nadan's mother brags about his 'future money.'"

He put the toy down too hard.

"Must be nice," Yoram went on. "To have everything figured out. To walk around like little Arkads while the rest of us are still trying not to starve."

The words stung because they weren't true, but they weren't exactly false either.

Bela bristled. "We're not walking around like anything," he said. "We still work. We still mess up. We just—"

"Have rules," Yoram said in a mocking tone. "I know. I've heard you under that palm tree. 'Save this, don't spend that, think of future you.'" He rolled his eyes. "Sounds like a boring way to live."

"Boring is better than broke," Bela shot back.

Yoram's eyes flashed.

"You sound rich," he said coldly. "Not in coins—yet. In your head. Like you're above everyone else. Careful, Bela. People don't like it."

He flipped a coin onto the stall like it was nothing, grabbed the toy, and walked away.

Bela stared after him, jaw tight.

"I hate him," he muttered.

"No, you don't," Nadan said quietly. "You hate how he made you feel."

Bela opened his mouth to argue, then shut it.

Because Nadan was right.

The comment spread like spilled oil.

Within a week, kids in the neighbourhood had invented a new tease:

"Careful, don't touch that, the **rich club** might charge you interest."

"Ask the bankers under the palm tree."

"Hey, First Coins, how many rules to buy a snack, ten?"

Some said it jokingly. Some said it with an edge.

At first, the four of them laughed it off.

But the words got under their skin.

One evening under the palm tree, Bela threw himself down and groaned.

"I'm done," he said. "No more saving. I'm going to spend every coin this week just to prove a point."

Karim snorted. "Prove what, exactly? That you can be as stressed as everyone else again?"

"That I'm not acting better than them," Bela said. "You didn't hear Yoram. He made it sound like we think we're kings."

"We don't," Nadan said. "We're just… trying not to drown."

"Try telling them that," Bela said. "All they see is: we say 'no' to some things. We talk about 'future us.' We help Rafi, so rumours start. Suddenly we're the rich ones, and it's a crime."

Daria had been quiet, watching a line of ants head toward a dropped crumb.

"Maybe the problem isn't what we're doing," she said. "Maybe it's what we *look like* we're doing."

"What do you mean?" Karim asked.

"We keep talking about rules and plans," Daria said. "We sit under this tree, making decisions while everyone else rushes around. From the outside, that can look like superiority, not survival. They don't see our fears. They see our tablets."

She smirked slightly. "And your loud mouth."

Bela glared. "I'm not loud."

All three of them looked at him.

"Okay, I'm loud," he admitted.

Nadan lay back, staring up at the palm leaves.

"Even before we had more coins," he said, "we started to think differently. About money, about time, about work. That makes us different. People always notice when someone is different."

Karim sighed. "So what do we do? Hide? Stop learning?"

"No," Daria said sharply. "We never stop learning. That's the one thing we *don't* give up because someone laughs."

"Then what?" Bela asked. "Just get used to being 'the rich club' even when we're not?"

Daria tapped her stylus against the clay.

"Maybe we need to answer a question we've been avoiding," she said. "We keep saying we want to be 'rich' one day. But what does that even mean?"

They went quiet.

They'd thrown the word around easily.

Rich like Arkad.

Rich like the landlord.

Rich like people who didn't panic when a jar broke or a job fell through.

But not once had they actually defined it.

The next day, they met near a quieter part of the river, away from the market noise.

Daria placed a blank tablet on her lap.

"All right," she said. "Let's do this properly. When you say you want to be rich, what are you really saying?"

"Gold," Bela said immediately. "Lots of it. Big piles. Heavy pouches. Maybe a chest."

Daria didn't write that down.

"Liar," she said. "You want more than that."

Bela frowned. "Fine. I want… to never feel like Rafi did. Like every coin already belongs to someone else. I want to be able to buy something nice for my parents without calculating whether we'll starve."

Daria wrote:

- Not being owned by debt
- Being able to be generous without panic

She looked at Karim.

"You?"

Karim stared at the slow-moving water.

"My parents fight about money," he said. "Quietly, but I hear it. I want enough that they don't have to. I want to be able to help them when they're old, not just watch them struggle."

He hesitated.

"And..." he added, "I want to be able to say 'no' sometimes. To a bad job, to a bad boss. To not be trapped because I need every single coin."

Daria wrote:

- Help family
- Freedom to say no to bad deals

"Nadan?" she asked.

Nadan took longer.

"I want... peace," he said finally. "I've watched my mother count coins with a tight jaw for years. I don't need a palace. I just want to know: the roof is safe, food is there, and if something breaks, it won't break us."

He paused.

"And," he added, surprising himself, "I want to understand money so well that I'm never fooled by it. I don't just want coins. I want clarity."

Daria wrote:

- Stability at home
- Understanding instead of fear

She turned the stylus on herself.

"As for me," she said, "I want choices. I've seen women whose whole life depends on a husband's mood. I want to be able to stand on my own feet if I have to. I want to choose who I marry, where I live, what I do, because I'm not desperate."

She added:

- Independence
- Choices

They stared at the list.

None of it mentioned fancy clothes.

None of it mentioned impressing Yoram.

"So we don't actually want to be 'rich,'" Karim said slowly. "We want security, freedom, and the ability to help."

"And nice snacks," Bela added. "Let's not lie."

Daria smiled and added a small note in the corner:

- (And some joy.)

"Good," she said. "Now we have a definition."

Bela looked unconvinced. "How does this help with people calling us the rich club?"

"Because we can answer the insult in our own heads," Daria said. "When someone says 'you're just trying to be rich,' we know what that really means: 'we're trying not to be scared all the time.'"

Karim exhaled. "That… helps," he admitted.

The real test came when success knocked louder.

It started with **Karim**.

His extra hours at the workshop paid off. His uncle, impressed, started giving him harder tasks and paying him a little more than a regular helper.

"You're not just carrying wood anymore," his uncle said.

"You're adding value. I pay for value."

Karim's income grew, not by a miracle, but by a noticeable amount.

He followed the rules: saved, invested a bit in the shield-maker, paid into his "Future Karim" stash.

He also did something else: he bought his mother a new cooking pot without waiting for a crisis.

"She cried," he told them under the palm tree, embarrassed. "She said no one's ever bought her something 'big' just because."

"That's rich," Daria said.

"I'm not rich," Karim protested.

"You gave without panicking," Daria said. "That's one of the things we wrote. So, yes. That's rich."

Next was **Bela**.

Word spread in the market that he was "exceptional" at attracting customers. His father bragged about him to other stall owners. One of them offered Bela a side deal: help sell his goods a few days a week for a share of the extra profit.

Bela suddenly had **two** streams of income.

He strutted a bit.

"Look at you," Daria said. "Multiple income sources. Fancy."

"Don't worry," Bela said. "I'll still complain like a poor man."

He did buy a new cloak, a good one, not ridiculously fancy, but clearly nicer.

That's when the whispers got louder.

"Must be nice," Yoram muttered as Bela walked past. "Money changes people."

"It changed his cloak," someone said.

"It'll change his friends next," another voice added.

Bela heard.

He laughed it off in front of them, but under the palm tree, his smile slipped.

"Do I look like I'm showing off?" he asked, pulling at the cloak. "Be honest."

"Yes," Daria said.

Karim elbowed her. "No," he said quickly. "You look... successful."

"There's a difference," Nadan added. "Showing off is when you buy things to make others feel small. You bought something that will last and makes you feel proud of your work. That's fine."

"But I hate how they look at me now," Bela said. "Like I've crossed some invisible line."

Nadan understood more than he said.

Because it was happening to him, too.

His master had begun paying him a little extra for important jobs. A merchant, impressed by how clearly one of Nadan's tablets was written, had tipped him personally.

"It saves me trouble," the man had said. "That's worth something."

Nadan's savings climbed faster.

He didn't change anything obvious. No new clothes, no fancy trinkets. But inside, he felt a dangerous new voice:

You're doing well.
 You're ahead.
 You're smarter than most of them.

He hated that voice.

It sounded too much like Yoram's accusation.

The moment everything almost snapped came from the last

person they expected.

It came from **Daria**.

Her father, impressed by her budgeting with oil and grain, had given her more control over their household accounts. She discovered she genuinely loved it, making numbers line up, planning, finding small ways to save here and invest there.

Her family's finances smoothed out.

Fewer surprises. Fewer panicky weeks.

Daria glowed with quiet pride.

Then one day, another girl from the neighbourhood, **Mina**, asked her for help.

"My mother is drowning in bills," Mina said. "She can't read. I can barely read. The moneylenders confuse her. Can you… look?"

Daria agreed.

She spent an afternoon in Mina's tiny house, going through crumpled tablets and half-explained debts. She did what she'd learned from Arkad's plan: listed everything, sorted it, helped Mina's mother see what was real and what was unfair.

"You don't owe this much," Daria said firmly, pointing to one tablet. "He's charging you extra on extra. This isn't right."

Mina's mother began to cry.

"Can you speak to him with us?" she asked.

So Daria did.

She went to the moneylender's stall with Mina and her mother, clay notes in hand. She spoke clearly and calmly, showing where the numbers didn't match, reminding him of the king's new rules.

He wasn't happy.

But with other customers listening, with the threat of the king's debt plan hanging over him, he agreed to adjust.

On the way home, Mina hugged Daria so hard she almost dropped her tablet.

"You're amazing," Mina said. "You saved us."

The words felt like sunshine.

Too much sunshine.

That evening under the palm tree, Daria told the story. By the end, she was talking faster, hands moving more, eyes shining.

"I could do this for more families," she said. "I understand this stuff. They don't. I could be… I don't know… a money advisor. A planner. People would pay for it."

"They should," Karim said. "You're good at it."

Bela grinned. "Daria the Money Master. I like it."

Daria's chin lifted a little higher.

"Maybe one day," she said, "I'll be richer than Arkad."

It was a joke.

Mostly.

The silence that followed told her friends it had landed differently.

They looked at her, then at each other, and something tense sat between them.

"Is that what you want?" Nadan asked softly. "To be richer than Arkad?"

"Why not?" Daria said, defensive. "He's not a god. He's just a man who learned early and made good choices. We're doing the same."

"Yes," Nadan said, "but he also… gives. Teaches. Tries to lift the whole city. When you say 'richer than Arkad,' are you thinking about that part, too?"

Daria opened her mouth, then closed it.

She realised suddenly that in her mind, "richer than Arkad" had looked like piles of gold, a big house, respect.

Not necessarily like spending hours in hot courtyards repeating the same lessons to stubborn people.

She felt her face heat up.

"I just meant—" she began.

"I know what you meant," Nadan said gently. "And it scared me. Because I heard a little piece of Yoram in there: 'Look at me. I'm above you.'"

The words hit harder because they came from him.

Daria bristled. "So I can't even be ambitious now? Is wanting to be successful suddenly evil?"

"No," Karim said quickly. "We just… don't want to become the people we used to complain about. The ones who look down on everyone else."

Daria slapped her stylus against the tablet.

"Do you all think I'm becoming that?" she asked.

No one answered.

Which answered enough.

She stood up abruptly.

"Fine," she said. "Maybe I should stop helping people with their money, too. Wouldn't want to look like I know anything."

She walked away before they could stop her.

The group felt broken.

For days, Daria avoided the palm tree. The boys met without her, the empty spot where she usually sat like a missing tooth.

"This is bad," Karim said. "We need her. And she needs us to make sure she doesn't drift into… whatever that was."

"Arrogance," Bela said quietly. "We're all flirting with it. Not just her."

Nadan nodded.

"I hear it in my own head," he admitted. "When I see people making terrible money choices, part of me thinks, 'How can they be so foolish?' And I have to remind myself: I was exactly like that not long ago."

"So what do we do?" Karim asked. "We can't just drag her back here."

"No," Nadan said. "But maybe someone else can help us see this more clearly. Someone who's actually rich and somehow not unbearable."

WHAT DOES "RICH" EVEN MEAN?

"You mean Arkad," Bela said.

"Yeah," Nadan said. "Him."

They didn't find him in the courtyard this time.

They found him in a smaller place: a quiet lane near a fig tree, talking with a young woman who was asking him about a business idea.

They waited until she left.

"Back again," Arkad said when he saw them. "How goes your journey?"

"We're... fighting," Bela blurted out.

Arkad smiled faintly. "That happens," he said. "What about?"

Nadan took a breath.

"About success," he said. "We've been doing what you said. Saving, investing, learning skills. It's starting to show. People call us 'rich' now, even when we're not. They resent us. And inside our own group, we're starting to feel proud, or jealous, or both."

He met Arkad's eyes.

"How do we do this," Nadan asked, "without becoming selfish... or hated?"

Arkad studied them for a moment.

"You have reached a dangerous part of the path," he said. "Many people fall here, not because they failed, but because they **succeeded a little** and let their hearts swell too much."

He folded his arms.

"Listen carefully," he said.

"There are **three kinds of 'rich'**:

1. Those who look rich.
2. Those who *are* rich but afraid.
3. Those who are rich in a way that also blesses others."

He ticked them off on his fingers.

"The first," he said, "spend to display. They buy to be seen. Their wealth is like a costume. If you stripped away the clothes and the parties, they would feel empty."

Bela shifted uncomfortably.

"The second," Arkad continued, "hoard. They save and save and never enjoy, never share. They are always afraid it will vanish. Their wealth is like a cage they sit in, counting bars."

Daria's empty place in the group seemed to flicker into existence for a second.

"The third," Arkad finished, "have enough for themselves, enough for their future, and enough to help others when they choose. They enjoy what they have without needing to prove anything. They don't feel bigger than others. They just feel… responsible."

He looked at Nadan.

"Which kind do you want to be?" he asked.

"Third," Nadan said immediately.

"Good," Arkad said. "Then remember this:

Money is a tool.
   A dangerous tool when your heart is twisted.
   A powerful tool when your heart is clear."

He turned to Bela.

"Your new cloak," he said. "Did you buy it to feel proud of your work, or to make Yoram feel small?"

Bela swallowed. "Both," he admitted.

Arkad smiled. "At least you are honest," he said. "Wear it. But check your heart when you put it on. If you feel the need to show it off, remember how it felt when others made you feel less."

He turned to Karim.

"You are helping your family," Arkad said. "That is good. But do not start measuring your worth only in how much you can give them. You are not a walking coin purse. You are a son, a brother, a person. Let money serve those roles. Not replace them."

Karim nodded, eyes wide.

Finally, Arkad spoke about Daria, even though she wasn't there.

"As for your friend who has discovered she is clever with money," he said, "do not punish her for that. The world needs people like her. But remind her, and yourselves, that the **goal** is not to stand on a hill and look down. It is to stand firmly enough that you can reach a hand to those still climbing."

He rested his hand briefly on Nadan's shoulder.

"Do you know why I teach in courtyards?" he asked. "It is not because I enjoy repeating myself. It is because being rich in a city full of desperate people is… unpleasant. Their fear and hunger eventually become your problem too. I teach so that more people can stand stronger. That, in the end, protects everyone, including me."

He stepped back.

"When people call you 'rich,'" he said, "you cannot control their jealousy. But you can control your reaction. You can say inside yourself:

'I am not rich **instead** of you.
    I am rich **so I can help**,
    and so I do not add to the problem.'"

He smiled.

"Walk humbly," he said. "But do not walk backwards to make others comfortable."

Then he left them standing in the lane, minds full.

The first person they talked to after that was Daria.

They found her in her courtyard, helping her father go through account tablets. When she saw them, her mouth tightened.

"You three again," she said. "Come to tell me I'm too ambitious?"

"No," Nadan said. "We came to tell you we're sorry."

She blinked.

"What?"

"We were scared," Karim said. "Not of you, really. Of what we could all turn into if we weren't careful."

Bela nodded. "We heard Arkad talk about three kinds of 'rich,'" he said. "The show-offs, the hoarders, and the helpers. We thought you were sliding toward the first or second. Maybe we were wrong. Maybe we were right. But we said it badly."

Daria's eyes softened just a fraction.

"What did he say we should be?" she asked.

"The third kind," Nadan said. "Rich enough to be stable, to help others, and to not need to prove anything. Using money like a tool, not a trophy."

Daria stared at the ground.

"Part of me liked the idea of being 'richer than Arkad,'" she admitted. "Not just in coins. In respect. In power. It scared me when you called it out, because… you weren't wrong."

She looked up, eyes fierce but clear.

"I still want to be very good with money," she said. "I still want to earn well, save well, and have choices. But you're right. I don't want to spend my life sitting on top of a pile of coins, guarding it from everyone. I want to be… like he is. Solid. Free. Useful."

"Then so do we," Karim said.

Bela grinned. "We can be annoying rich people together."

Daria smacked his shoulder. "We can be **useful** rich people together," she corrected.

They laughed.

The tension leaked away, like water slipping out of a cracked jar.

Back under the palm tree, Daria wrote a new page.

At the top, she titled it:

What "Rich" Means To Us

Underneath, she listed:

- Enough for **basic needs** without constant panic.
- Enough saved and invested for **future us** to be safe.
- Enough skill to keep earning honestly.
- Enough extra to **help others** sometimes, by choice.
- And the discipline **not** to spend just to impress.

At the bottom, she added:

"If we forget this, we become the people we used to be afraid of."

They all pressed their thumbs onto the clay, leaving marks around the words.

It wasn't a legal contract.

But it might have been the most important promise they'd

made so far.

Life in Babylon didn't get easier overnight.

People still gossiped. Some still called them the rich club. Yoram still made snide comments.

The difference was inside.

When Nadan heard "rich" used like a weapon, he quietly translated it to his own definition.

When Bela caught himself bragging, he thought about the three kinds of rich and shut his mouth.

When Karim felt guilty for wanting more, he remembered that wanting security and the ability to help wasn't greed, it was responsibility.

When Daria helped another family with their accounts, she reminded herself: *This isn't about proving I'm smart. It's about making one less person afraid.*

Slowly, the word that had felt like an accusation turned into something else:

Not a badge.

Not an insult.

A job.

10

The Bag That Wasn't Theirs

It happened on the most ordinary morning.

The sun was just starting to burn off the mist over Babylon's walls. Merchants dragged open shutters, kids chased each other between stalls, and Nadan was running across the square because, as usual, he was a little late.

He nearly tripped over the bag.

It was sitting in the dust near a pillar. Not hidden. Not guarded. Just… there.

If he hadn't stumbled, he might have missed it completely. As it was, he only just caught himself before face-planting.

"Ow," he muttered, rubbing his toe.

Then he saw it.

A thick, brown leather bag, tied with a cord. Heavy.

He looked around automatically.

No one seemed to be searching the ground. No one was patting their belt with a panicked face. The crowd flowed around him, busy and uninterested.

"Did anyone lose a bag?" Nadan called out, holding it up.

A few people glanced over, shrugged, kept moving.

The bag felt heavy.

Too heavy for bread. Too heavy for cloth scraps. The kind of heavy that made your heart beat weirdly just from holding it.

Nadan's fingers tightened around it.

Coins, a little voice whispered in his head.

He swallowed.

Probably coins.

He didn't open it.

Not there, in the middle of the square.

He tied the cord tighter and tucked the bag into his belt, hidden under his robe, then walked away as calmly as he could manage.

His mind wasn't calm at all.

Someone dropped it.
  Someone needs it.
  Someone might be crying right now.

And at the same time:

What if no one claims it?
  What if no one saw me pick it up?
  What if this is... a sign?

By the time he reached the palm tree, he felt sick.

Bela was already there, practising his "merchant voice" on a confused pigeon.

"You there! Sir! Yes, you with the feathers—" He stopped when he saw Nadan's face. "You look like you stole something."

"I think someone else did," Nadan said, dropping down and carefully placing the bag between them.

Bela's eyes went wide.

"What is that?" he asked.

"I found it near the square," Nadan said. "No one claimed it. It's heavy."

Karim arrived next, then Daria. It took about ten seconds for everyone to be sitting in a tight circle, staring at the bag like it might explode.

"Did you look inside?" Daria asked.

"No," Nadan said.

"Why not?" Bela blurted.

"Because I wanted witnesses," Nadan said. "If I opened it alone and it's full of gold, I didn't trust my own brain."

Daria nodded slowly. "That's... actually smart."

"Can we look now?" Karim asked.

"Yes," Nadan said. "Together."

His fingers shook slightly as he loosened the cord.

He opened the bag just enough to peek inside.

The others leaned in.

Inside were **coins**.

A lot of them.

Not all gold, mostly silver, some copper, but a few shining yellow pieces that made Nadan's breath catch. He couldn't count them all in one glance, but it was more money than any of them had ever seen loose and unguarded.

Bela let out a low whistle.

"That," he said, "is definitely heavy."

Daria's eyes were serious, not greedy.

"Close it," she said.

Nadan snapped the bag shut.

They sat in silence for a moment, all of them feeling the same electric thought they didn't want to admit:

If we kept this, we would be "rich" in the easy way. Right now.

Karim broke the silence.

"Okay," he said. "So. Arkad's rules, our rules, and every story our parents ever told us say one thing: this is **not** ours. We need to return it."

Bela nodded. "Of course," he said quickly. "Obviously. Definitely."

No one mentioned that his voice was a little too fast.

Daria tilted her head, studying the three of them.

"Let's say it clearly," she said. "We are not keeping this. Right?"

"Right," Nadan said.

"Right," Karim said.

Bela hesitated for a fraction of a second.

"...Right," he said.

Daria watched him.

"Out loud," she said. "What are you thinking?"

Bela threw up his hands. "Fine," he said. "I'm thinking: what if we use it *temporarily*? Hear me out. We invest it with the shield-maker or some other safe thing. We make it grow. Then we return the original amount and keep the extra. That way no one loses, and we gain."

Karim stared at him.

"That's not 'hear me out,'" he said. "That's 'hear me talk myself into theft in a clever way.'"

"It's not theft," Bela protested. "We'd pay it back!"

"Without asking," Daria said. "Without permission. With a risk that something goes wrong and the owner gets nothing. That's... exactly what bad lenders do, Bela. They play with other people's money for their own gain."

Bela winced.

"Besides," Nadan added quietly, "we built our whole system, First Coins, rules, everything—on trust. Trust in ourselves. Trust that we won't cheat even when we could. If we fail this test, what are we even doing?"

"That's what this is, isn't it?" Karim said. "A test. To see if everything we've learned matters when no one's watching."

They all looked at the bag.

No name on the outside. No sign, no symbol.

Just a heavy temptation sitting in the dust between friends.

"So how do we find the owner?" Bela asked. "We can't stand in the square all day yelling 'who dropped a bag of money' unless we want half the city to claim it."

"He's right," Daria said. "If we ask in the wrong way, we'll get liars. We need… information."

"Maybe there's something inside," Karim suggested. "A note? A mark on one of the coins? Something."

Nadan frowned, then carefully opened the bag again, this time tipping some of the contents gently onto Daria's spare cloth.

Most of the coins were ordinary, worn from use.

But near the bottom, they found something different:

A small clay token with a symbol pressed into it—a stylised **fish** and a number. Someone's mark.

"Could be a merchant seal," Nadan said. "Or a house mark."

Daria turned it over.

"I've seen this," she said slowly. "On sacks near the river. I think it belongs to one of the fish traders."

"Which one?" Bela asked.

She closed her eyes, picturing the symbol.

"There's a big stall by the east gate," she said. "Seller named **Hadad**, I think. His crates have a mark like this."

"Then we start there," Nadan said.

They carefully scooped the coins back into the bag, leaving the clay token out so Daria could study it as they walked.

Finding Hadad wasn't hard.

His stall smelled like the sea and shouted like a marketplace all by itself.

"Fresh catch! Best in Babylon! If it smelled any fresher, it would still be swimming!" he boomed, waving a fish dramatically in the air.

Crates behind him bore the same fish symbol as the clay token.

They waited until the crowd thinned, then approached.

"Sir," Nadan said, "can we ask you something?"

"Ask me to lower prices and the answer is no," Hadad said cheerfully. "Ask me about fish and you'll get a speech."

Daria held up the clay token.

"Is this your mark?" she asked.

Hadad's expression changed.

"Yes," he said. "Why do you have it?"

"We found this," Nadan said, carefully placing the heavy bag on the stall.

Hadad's eyes widened.

"Where?" he demanded.

"In the square," Nadan said. "We didn't open it fully in public, but when we saw the token, we thought it might be yours. Or your employer's."

Hadad looked like someone had just handed him his own heart.

"This is my supplier's money," he said hoarsely. "He wears his token on his bags in case of loss. We were due to pay the sailors today. I was supposed to deliver this bag to him this evening." His face went pale. "It must have fallen from my wagon."

He opened the bag fully now, counted quickly, then sagged with relief.

"All there," he breathed. "Blessed is god... all there."

He looked at the four of them as if seeing them for the first time.

"You brought it back," he said with a hint of surprise.

"Of course," Daria said.

Hadad swallowed.

"Do you know what would have happened if someone else found it? If a less honest person had picked it up?" he asked. "My name would be ruined. My supplier would think I'd stolen it. I might have lost my stall."

Karim shivered. He could see it: one accident, one missing bag, one man's whole life uprooted.

"We just thought it should go back," Nadan said.

Hadad stared at them a moment longer, then reached into the bag, took out a handful of coins, and held them out.

"This is yours," he said. "A reward. You deserve ten times this."

Bela's eyes widened.

The amount in Hadad's hand was not small.

Nadan's heart did a strange double-beat. They hadn't done this for a reward. But they *did* have goals. Family needs. Future money.

Daria's voice cut through the sudden heat in his face.

"We can't take that," she said.

Hadad frowned. "Why not? You saved me."

"Because it's not your money," Daria said. "It's your supplier's. You still have debts, payments, responsibilities. We won't be the reason your accounts get unbalanced. If he wants to reward us after you explain what happened, he can. But we won't take it from this bag."

Hadad stared at her.

Then, slowly, he smiled.

"You're very powerful," he said. "In a good way."

He put the coins back.

"How about this," he said. "You four come back tomorrow

evening, after I've spoken to my supplier. If he agrees, we'll reward you from *our* pockets. Not this bag."

"That feels right," Daria said.

The others nodded.

As they walked away, Bela half-whispered, half-groaned, "We just said no to money. Again. This is becoming a bad habit."

Karim laughed. "A useful one," he said. "Old us would have grabbed it without a thought."

"Old us might have grabbed the whole bag," Nadan added.

They all shuddered a little.

The next day dripped by slowly.

Every time Nadan heard coins clink at the scribe's table, he thought of the bag. Every time Bela made a sale, he imagined what he could have done with that rushed reward.

"New sandals," he muttered at one point. "New cloak. Savings. Future cloak savings."

"Future Bela would approve," Karim said dryly.

Daria mostly stayed quiet.

"I keep replaying it in my head," she admitted under the palm tree. "What if we'd kept it? We could have moved faster. Bought more flour, more wood, more tools. It's tempting."

"But then?" Nadan asked.

"Then every medal we hang around our neck would be tied to a stolen ribbon," Daria said. "Even if no one else saw it, we would."

She looked at the others.

"We talk a lot about being 'rich' one day," she said. "I realise something yesterday: if getting there requires us to become thieves or liars, I don't want it."

"Me neither," Karim said.

Bela sighed. "Same," he said. "Even if my snack budget disagrees."

They laughed, tension breaking.

The next evening, they returned to Hadad's stall.

He greeted them with a grin so wide it nearly split his beard.

"My supplier almost fainted when I told him," Hadad said.

"His face! You should have seen it."

"I told him about you. He wanted to meet you, but business

took him away. He said: 'Give those honest kids whatever you think is fair. They saved both of us.'"

He reached under the stall and brought out a smaller pouch.

"This," he said, "is from both of us. From our profit. Not just his bag. You will not make us poorer. You will make us grateful."

He handed it to Nadan.

It was a lot lighter than the first bag, but still not trivial.

Nadan didn't argue.

"We accept," he said. "Thank you."

Hadad nodded. "I hope my own children grow to be like you," he said. "Now go before I give you all my fish too."

They laughed and stepped away.

Under the palm tree, they opened the new pouch.

It wasn't life-changing money.

But it was more than they usually saw at once.

"Now what?" Karim asked.

"We saved a man's job," Bela said. "I say we blow it all on the biggest feast in Babylon."

"Try again," Daria said.

They went quiet, then started turning it over like they did every decision.

"Part of it should go to our First Coins," Nadan said. "We earned this honestly. It's income like any other."

"Agreed," Daria said. "Some for savings, some for investing, some for future us."

"And some for joy," Bela said. "Come on. Even you wrote that down in the 'What Rich Means' list."

Daria smiled reluctantly. "Fine," she said. "We can use a small part to celebrate. But not to show off, just to mark that we passed a test."

"A trust test," Karim said.

He thought for a moment, then added, "Maybe we should give a piece to someone else, too. Not as 'Look at us, we're generous,' but as 'This blessing passed through us, not just to us.'"

They all liked that.

In the end, they divided the reward like this:

- A portion to their individual savings (First Coins).
- A portion to try one new, careful investment idea together.

- A small portion to buy bread, fruit, and a bit of sweet drink and have a quiet feast by the river.
- And a portion, they decided, to quietly slip to someone who needed it more, Rafi, or Mina's family, or someone else they'd seen struggling that week.

Not as heroes.

As channels.

The feast by the river wasn't grand.

Just simple food, eaten sitting on the ground, watching the water turn orange in the sunset.

But it tasted different.

"Is it just me," Bela said, chewing happily, "or does this feel better than if we'd spent stolen money?"

"It's not just you," Nadan said.

Karim nodded. "This feels… clean," he said. "Light."

Daria looked at the pouch with the remaining coins.

"Do you realise what happened?" she said. "We had a chance to jump ahead by breaking our own rules. We said no. And we still ended up ahead, maybe slower, but without regret."

"Not every story ends like that," Karim said. "Sometimes doing the right thing costs you."

"True," Daria said. "But even then, there's something we keep that doesn't fit in a pouch."

"What?" Bela asked.

She tapped her chest.

"Trust," she said. "From others. From ourselves."

They sat in silence, listening to the water.

Nadan thought about how it would have felt if they'd kept the bag. The constant fear of being discovered. The shame, even if no one ever knew. The way every coin earned afterward would have been built on that crack.

Instead, he felt… solid.

Their path was still slow. Their coins still few.

But their **foundation** was stronger.

Later, as they walked home through the dim streets, Nadan remembered something Arkad had once said:

"Better a little wealth that sits on strong honesty
 than a mountain of gold balanced on a lie."

FIRST COINS

He hadn't really understood it before.

Now he did.

They'd just chosen the kind of rich they wanted to be.

And it didn't start with a bag of coins.

It started with four friends under a palm tree, deciding, again and again, who they wanted to become, even when no one else was watching.

11

The Test of a Hundred Coins

The king's challenge started as a rumour and turned into a storm.

At first, it was just whispers in the market:

"The king is tired of people complaining they're poor."
 "They say he asked Arkad to prove his ideas work on anyone."
 "There's going to be… a test."

By midday, it wasn't whispers anymore.

A royal messenger stood in the main square, voice ringing out over the crowd:

"By command of the king of Babylon!

A group of citizens shall be chosen.
 Each will receive **one hundred silver coins** from the royal

treasury.

After **one year**, they must return to show what has become of the money and themselves.

Some will waste it. Some will keep it. Some may grow it.
The king wishes to learn **why**."

The crowd buzzed like a shaken beehive.

"Free money?" someone shouted.
"It's a trap," another muttered.
"I bet Arkad is behind this," said a third.

He was.

That evening, the four friends sat under their palm tree, hearts pounding.

"One hundred silver coins," Bela said, eyes wide. "Do you know how much that is? It's like a mountain compared to our usual…"

"Don't drool," Daria said. "It's not a gift. It's a test."

Karim frowned. "Do you think we'd even be chosen?" he asked. "Babylon has thousands of people."

Nadan shrugged, trying to sound calm. "We might. We go to Arkad's talks. We've been trying his rules. If he needs test subjects…"

Bela grinned. "We're test subjects now. Fancy."

"You're a test subject," Daria said dryly. "Specifically, 'What happens if we give this boy too much energy?'"

They laughed, but the question hung between them:

What would we do if it really was us?

They didn't have to wonder for long.

Two days later, as Nadan was leaving the scribe's workshop, someone called his name.

"Nadan, son of Baruk?"

He turned to see a royal messenger and one of Arkad's servants.

"Yes," Nadan said, suddenly nervous.

"You are requested," the messenger said, "at Arkad's house tomorrow morning, with your three friends. Bela, Karim, and Daria."

Nadan's heart jumped.

"All of us?" he asked.

"Those names," the messenger said. "Don't be late."

He walked away, leaving Nadan staring after him, brain racing.

It's us, he thought. *We're in it.*

They gathered at the palm tree that evening.

"We're not ready," Karim said immediately.

"We've been preparing for this all year," Daria replied. "We just didn't know it."

Bela paced in a small circle.

"Okay, ground rules," he said. "If we get money, we do **not** immediately buy everything we've ever wanted."

"Agreed," Nadan said.

"Even though I really, really want to," Bela added.

"Also agreed," Nadan said.

Daria took a deep breath.

"Let's imagine the worst-case scenario," she said. "The king gives us each one hundred silver. If we blow it, we don't just fail ourselves. We tell him Arkad's lessons don't work. We make him look like a liar."

Silence.

That was heavier than the coins.

"I don't want to be the reason people stop listening to him," Karim said quietly.

"Then we won't be," Daria said. "We already know the rules. Save. Invest wisely. Avoid traps. Think of future us. Grow our earning. Use our home well. Face reality."

She squeezed the clay tablet in her lap.

"Tomorrow," she said, "we just… do all of that with a bigger number."

"Just," Bela echoed. "Sure. No pressure."

Arkad's courtyard was different the next morning.

Smaller group. No random onlookers. Maybe twenty people in all, young, old, men, women. Some Nadan recognised from the talks. Others were strangers.

A table stood near the centre, and on it, in neat stacks, were bags.

Not as big as the fish trader's bag. But still heavy-looking.

Arkad sat on his usual stone seat, with a royal official beside him.

"Friends," Arkad said, "today, the king has given us an opportunity—and a risk."

He gestured to the bags.

"In each of these," he said, "are **one hundred silver coins**. The king wishes to see, after **one year**, what different people do with the same amount."

The royal official spoke next.

"This is not a gift," he said. "At the end of the year, each of you must return here. We will ask:

- How much of the hundred is left?
- What has it become?
- What have you learned?"

He looked around.

"You will not be punished if you lose it," he said. "But you will be... questioned."

His meaning was clear.

Arkad stood again.

"I recommended you all," he said. "Some of you have been learning. Some are new. The king wants variety."

His eyes landed briefly on Nadan, Bela, Daria, and Karim. There was no smile this time, just a steady look that said, *This is real now.*

"Remember," Arkad said, "the coins are simple. It is your choices that are complex."

One by one, people were called to the table.

"Daria, daughter of Rahim."
  "Karim, son of Yusef."
  "Bela, son of Oman."
  "Nadan, son of Baruk."

Each stepped forward, received a bag, and spoke their name to the scribe, who recorded everything on a large tablet.

The weight of the purse in Nadan's hands felt unreal.

He'd never held that much before.

It would have been easy to get drunk on the feeling.

Instead, he heard Arkad's voice in his mind:

Reality. Respect it.

He bowed slightly, stepped back, and joined his friends at the edge of the courtyard.

They didn't talk much on the walk to the palm tree.

Each felt the weight at their belt.

Finally Bela exploded.

"This is insane," he said. "I feel like I'm walking with a thunderstorm in my pouch."

"Same," Karim said. "Every pickpocket in Babylon suddenly looks ten times more dangerous."

"The money is the easy part," Daria said. "What we do with it is what matters."

Nadan nodded.

"So we do what we always do," he said. "We meet. We think. We don't rush."

He put his bag down on the ground between them.

"First question," he said. "Is this **shared** or **separate**? Do we combine our coins into one plan or treat them as four different tests?"

Bela looked at the bag, then at his own.

"I vote shared," he said. "We've always been stronger together."

Karim agreed. "We trust each other," he said. "Four minds are less likely to be stupid than one."

"Usually," Daria said.

Nadan thought carefully.

THE TEST OF A HUNDRED COINS

"The king is testing individuals," he said. "But he didn't say we can't work together. If anything, Arkad has always encouraged sharing ideas. I say we make one plan, but keep our accounts separate, so we can explain clearly what happened with each bag."

"Deal," Daria said.

They tipped all four bags out into the middle.

Four hundred silver coins.

The sight made Nadan's chest tighten.

"So," Daria said, steadying her voice, "what do we **not** do?"

"Gamble," Karim said.

"Throw feasts to impress people," Bela added, glancing at himself.

"Lend it all to one unproven trader," Nadan said. "Or to any one person, really."

"Correct," Daria said. "And what **must** we do?"

"Save a part, no matter what," Karim said.

"Use some to increase our earning ability," Nadan added. "Tools, training, things that make more money over time."

"Invest some in safe, tested places," Daria said. "Like we did with the shield-maker. Maybe new ones too, but carefully."

"And set aside part for Future Us," Bela said. "Even if it's tempting not to."

They were quiet for a moment.

"Let's break it into parts," Daria said at last, drawing in the dirt.

"Four hundred coins total.

- Part 1: **Learning & tools** – things that make us more valuable.
- Part 2: **Investments** – money working in safe ways.
- Part 3: **Family & home** – small improvements that help long-term.
- Part 4: **Future us** – locked away for later.
- Part 5: **Joy** – we're humans, not donkeys."

"Donkeys like joy too," Bela said.

"Noted," Daria replied.

They argued for hours.

Not angrily—intensely.

"How much goes into learning?"
"What's 'safe enough' as an investment?"

"Are we allowed to help our families with this, or is that 'cheating' the test?"

In the end, they agreed:

- **30%** (120 coins) to safe-ish investments they understood: shield-maker expansion, a grain merchant with a good reputation, and part in Hadad's fish trade on clear terms.
- **25%** (100 coins) to **tools and learning**:
- A better set of carpentry tools and a payment to Karim's uncle so he could spend more time teaching instead of just using Karim as cheap labour.
- A small writing and numbers course with a retired accountant for Nadan and Daria.
- A simple stall setup for Bela so he could test running his own tiny side-business instead of always working under others.
- **20%** (80 coins) toward modest but real **family/home improvements**:
- Extra roof repairs and a slightly better oven for Nadan's house to support the bread-selling.
- A proper storage chest for Karim's family to protect their few valuables.
- Grain storage upgrades for Daria's family.
- Some stall improvements for Bela's parents.
- **15%** (60 coins) to **Future Us**:
- Split evenly, carefully recorded, invested in the safest, dullest way possible, small loans to strong, stable people and maybe a little in land-rent if they could find a trustworthy way.
- **10%** (40 coins) to **joy**:

- A few small gifts. A family meal that wasn't in crisis. Maybe one or two things they'd dreamed of that would last and not just disappear in a day.

"Is this perfect?" Daria asked when the numbers settled.

"No," Nadan said. "But it's honest. It uses everything we've learned."

"And it feels like us," Karim added.

Bela smiled slowly.

"And it still has snacks in it," he said. "So I approve."

The year that followed felt like three years squeezed into one.

There were **wins**:

Karim's new tools and training meant his uncle trusted him with full projects sooner. Together, they took on a big order for tables from a new tavern. Part of the profit went right back into the repayment plan for the king's money.

Nadan and Daria's extra lessons with the retired accountant unlocked whole new parts of the world. They learned how to track profits and losses, how to plan for irregular income, how to spot subtle cheating in contracts.

"This is like seeing in the dark," Daria said once, eyes shining.

Bela's stall experiment was chaotic but promising. He bought a small set of simple goods with part of their "learning" budget and tested different ways of selling, tracking what worked and what was just noise.

"I'm not just guessing anymore," he said. "I test, measure, adjust. I sound like Daria. It's terrifying."

There were **problems**, too:

The fish trade had a bad month when a storm delayed one shipment. Profits were smaller than they'd hoped. Their investment wasn't a disaster, but it wasn't magical either.

The grain merchant they trusted got sick for two months, slowing business. Their returns waited patiently with him until he recovered. It reminded them that even good people can hit trouble.

Nadan's family had an unexpected cost when his younger brother fell from a wall and broke his arm. Some of the "family/home" coins went there instead of to planned upgrades. No one regretted it.

There were **temptations**:

New clothes in the market displays. Friends inviting them to small luxuries "since you're doing well now." Yoram waving his coins around after getting a lucky windfall and saying, "See? I didn't need Arkad's rules."

They stuck to their plan.

Not perfectly.

But well.

They made mistakes.

They corrected them.

They kept going.

Full year later, standing again in Arkad's courtyard, they hardly recognised some of the faces around them.

Some of the other "test group" members looked crushed.

One man's eyes were hollow. A woman clutched an empty purse and stared at the ground.

Others looked nervous but okay.

A few, very few, seemed calm.

Arkad and the royal official took turns calling people forward.

One man admitted he'd blown almost everything in the first few months, gifts, parties, a new cloak, a gamble that went wrong. Now he had almost nothing and a sickening understanding of his own impulses.

THE TEST OF A HUNDRED COINS

A woman kept most of the money in a jar, too afraid to use it. "I have almost the whole 100 still," she said, "but... nothing more." No growth. No learning. Just fear.

Another man had tried three "sure deals" from enthusiastic friends. Lost almost all of it. "I thought I could be clever in one year," he said bitterly. "Turns out I needed wisdom more than money."

Finally, their names were called.

"Daria, daughter of Rahim.
   Karim, son of Yusef.
   Bela, son of Oman.
   Nadan, son of Baruk."

They stepped forward together.

Arkad looked at them with open curiosity, not assumption.

"Well?" he asked. "What has the year done to your hundred?"

Daria spoke for them, but all four had prepared.

"We didn't treat it as prize money," she said. "We treated it as... a seed. We divided it with a plan: investments, skills, family, future, and a little joy."

The royal official leaned forward. "Numbers," he said crisply.

Daria nodded.

"First," she said, "We tracked each person's hundred separately, but we made decisions as a group and invested some of it together. At the end of the year:

- Each of us still has the **full 100** we were given.
- In addition, from earnings and investments using that 100, each has made a **profit**, though not the same amount."

She listed them, one by one.

Karim's extra carpentry work had earned him enough to not only return the hundred but also add to his family's savings and the repayment of their small family debts.

Bela's stall experiments had generated irregular but real profit. More importantly, he'd gained proof he could bring value to any trade.

Nadan and Daria's improved skills had resulted in extra pay, small advisory jobs, and one contract correction that saved a merchant from a bad deal, earning them a generous thank-you.

"If you combine our four hundreds," Daria concluded, "we started with **400 silver coins**. Altogether, counting what we still have and what we built because of it, we now hold the equivalent of about **600**, some in coins, some in tools, some in stronger family homes and better earning power."

She swallowed, suddenly aware of how big that sounded aloud.

Arkad's eyes crinkled.

"So," he said, "the king gave you silver, and you turned it into silver, skill, stability, and hope."

He looked at the royal official.

"I think," he said, "this proves the point."

The official wasn't emotional, but even he nodded slowly.

He turned to the group.

"What was the hardest part?" he asked.

"Not spending," Bela said without hesitation. "Especially at the start, when it felt like we had more than we'd ever see again."

"The waiting," Karim added. "Investments take time. Skills take time. It's hard to put money into the ground and not dig it up every day to check if it's grown."

"Facing reality," Daria said. "There were times when deals were worse than we'd hoped, or costs higher than we'd planned. We had to adjust instead of pretending everything was fine."

Nadan thought for a moment.

"Remembering that the test wasn't really about the king," he said softly. "It was about us. We could have lied. We could have hidden losses. But then we'd only be fooling ourselves."

Arkad nodded, clearly pleased.

He raised his voice so everyone in the courtyard could hear.

"The king's experiment has shown us what my teachers taught me long ago:

- Money given to those with **no rules** disappears.
- Money kept by those ruled by **fear** does not grow.
- Money in the hands of those who **save, learn, plan, and act slowly** can grow—even if they start with nothing."

He looked at them one by one.

"You four did not perform magic," he said. "You followed simple steps. You will make bigger mistakes later. But you now know, in your bones, that this works."

The royal official stepped forward.

"By the king's order," he said, "those who grew their hundred may **keep their profit**. The original hundred must be returned, so the treasury stays whole."

He looked at the four friends.

"And in your case," he added, "the king has decided to let you keep **half** of your original hundreds as well."

They blinked.

"What?" Bela said.

"Fifty silver coins each," the official clarified. "You have proved you do not treat the king's money lightly. He wishes to see what you do next."

Bela opened his mouth, then closed it.

For once, he had nothing to say.

Much later, under the palm tree with their new, smaller but still precious pouches, they sat in stunned silence.

"We... passed," Karim said at last.

"And got a bonus level," Bela added weakly.

Daria stared at the pouch in her hands.

"This feels different," she said. "The hundred we received felt like pressure. This fifty feels like... trust."

"From the king," Nadan said. "From Arkad. From ourselves."

They didn't rush into new plans that day.

They just sat there, letting the victory sink in, not the coins, but the fact that a whole year of boring, steady, thoughtful choices had been seen, measured, and respected.

Bela finally broke the silence.

"You know what I realised?" he said. "We're not the Empty Pockets Club, and we're not the Rich Club either."

"What are we then?" Karim asked.

Bela thought.

"We're the **Builders Club**," he said. "We're not chasing coins. We're building something, inside us, around us."

Daria didn't laugh.

"I like that," she said.

Nadan smiled.

"So do I," he said. "Because coins can be lost. Skills can fade. Houses can fall. But if we keep building our *habits* and *character* like this…"

He tapped his chest.

"…then no matter what happens, we'll know how to start again."

They pressed their thumbs into the clay once more, under a new heading:

We are builders.
   Not just of money, but of lives.

The sun dipped behind Babylon's walls, casting long shadows.

Their future still held uncertainty, hard days, and mistakes.

But they knew this much:

They'd faced a bag that wasn't theirs, a city's jealousy, a friend's debt, a king's test, and their own pride, and they were still on the path.

The path wasn't glamorous.

It was just:

Save.
   Learn.
   Plan.
   Act.
   Repeat.

The kind of path that, over years, quietly turns ordinary teenagers into something rare:

People who understand money—

—and more importantly, people money can **trust**.

12

Full Circle

The first thing you would have noticed about Babylon, ten years later, was that it didn't look that different.

Same walls.
Same busy gates.
Same market noise.

But if you watched closely, some things had changed.

Especially under one particular palm tree.

A skinny kid paced back and forth in its shade, muttering to himself.

"Save... something," he said. "Don't spend everything. That's what he said, right? And then... invest? But in what? I don't even know where to start."

He flopped down onto the packed earth and groaned.

"I'm doomed."

"Terrible opening line," someone said.

The boy looked up.

A man in his late twenties stood there, carrying a worn clay tablet and a small bag at his belt. His tunic was plain but well-made, and his eyes had the kind of calm you didn't see often.

"Sorry," the boy said. "I'm just… talking to myself."

"Good," the man said. "You're decent company."

The boy frowned. "Do I know you?"

"Probably not," the man said. "But I know that look. It's the 'money keeps slipping away and I don't know what to do with my future' look."

The boy narrowed his eyes. "You a moneylender?" he asked suspiciously.

The man laughed. "No," he said. "I'm a scribe. And… something like an advisor. Name's Nadan."

The boy's eyebrows shot up. "You're **that** Nadan? The one who helped with the king's test? My uncle talks about you. Says you 'think too much but you're usually right.'"

"I'll take that as a compliment," Nadan said.

He sat down under the tree, not too close, not too far.

"So," he asked, "want to tell me why you're arguing with the dust?"

The boy hesitated, then sighed.

"I'm **Eli**" he said. "I run messages. I get coins. Somehow, they disappear. Everyone says, 'Be smart with money,' but no one explains what that actually means. Just 'Don't be stupid.' Not helpful."

"That's fair," Nadan said. "Telling someone 'Don't be stupid' is not a strategy."

He thought for a moment.

"What do you want?" he asked. "Really. Not 'more money.' What does 'better' look like for you?"

Eli picked at the dirt.

"I don't want to be rich like show-off rich," he said slowly. "I just… I don't want to panic every time I lose a job. I don't want to feel like one bad week means we're ruined. And… if I have kids one day, I don't want them to grow up scared of markets and landlords."

Nadan smiled faintly.

"That's almost exactly what I said under this tree," he said.

Eli blinked. "What?"

"Never mind," Nadan said. "Look, you're not doomed. You're just missing a map. Someone should have given you one years ago."

He set the clay tablet on his knee and started drawing simple circles.

"Here's the short version," he said. "No fancy words. No mystery."

He drew **seven** small symbols: a coin, a hammer, a lock, a house, a tiny old man's face, a rising line, and a heart.

"These," he said, "are the things that changed my life. And my friends' lives. And Rafi's. And half the people who listened instead of rolling their eyes."

Eli leaned in despite himself.

"I'm listening," he said.

"Good," Nadan said. "First:"

1. The First Coin

He tapped the coin symbol.

"Always keep **at least one coin out of ten** you earn," he said. "Don't give it to food, rent, treats, friends, or 'emergencies' that are really bad planning. That first part is **yours**. For your future."

Eli made a face. "I barely have enough as it is."

"Same story I told Arkad," Nadan said. "Same answer he gave me: if you always end with zero, keeping one in ten means you end with more than zero. You can survive on nine coins out of ten, because you've been surviving on ten out of ten and still ending broke."

Eli frowned, then slowly nodded.

"Painful," he said. "But... okay."

2. The Spending Test

Nadan tapped the hammer.

"Second," he said. "Learn the difference between *needs* and *wants*."

He began listing with his stylus:

- Food that keeps you healthy = **need**
- Basic shelter = **need**
- Sandals that don't fall apart = mostly **need**
- Extra sweets, show-off clothes, every party = **want**

"Nothing wrong with wants," Nadan said. "But if you always feed them first, your needs and future self starve. You can't out-earn bad habits. You have to **choose** where your coins go."

Eli sighed. "So no fun ever."

"Wrong," Nadan said. "Fun—yes. Constant, mindless fun—no. In our club, we always left a slice for joy. We just made sure that slice didn't eat the whole loaf."

3. Coins That Work

He tapped the rising line.

"Third," he said. "Once you have some saved, don't let it just sit forever. Put it somewhere it can **earn**."

"Like lending?" Eli asked. "Or… gambling?"

"Gambling is just a fancy way to donate to people who own dice," Nadan said. "Lending can work, **if** you understand who you lend to and what they'll do with it."

He ticked off on his fingers.

"Good signs," he said.

- The person has done this work successfully **before**.
- You understand the trade: shields, grain, cloth, not 'mysterious foreign jewels.'
- There is a clear plan and timing for repayment.

- If something goes wrong, there is still a way for them to pay you back slowly.

"Bad signs," he added.

- 'Double your money fast' with no risk explained.
- They won't share your risk, if it fails, **you** lose, they don't.
- You don't understand how exactly the profit appears.

"Your coins are your workers," he said. "Don't send them to work for fools or liars."

4. Guarding the Gate

He tapped the lock symbol.

"Fourth," he said. "Protect your money from **loss you could have avoided**."

"You mean like thieves?" Eli asked.

"Thieves, sure," Nadan said. "But also your own greed."

He told the short version of the purple cloth trader story, no long details, just enough: big promises, little safety, a 'limited time offer' that turned out to be mostly risk.

"We almost fell for it," he said. "Our greed dressed up as 'opportunity.' Arkad taught us: if you would be **shocked** to lose the money, you're not ready for that risk."

Eli chewed his lip. "So if I'd be devastated to lose ten coins, I shouldn't put ten into something risky?"

"Exactly," Nadan said. "Start smaller. Test people. Test deals. Don't test your whole future on one shiny promise."

5. Home as a Helper

He tapped the little house.

"Fifth," he said. "When you can, make your home part of your strength, not just a payment."

"I don't own a home," Eli said. "We rent a room behind a shop. It leaks."

"Same," Nadan said. "Back then, anyway. Owning came later. But even before that, we learned to use our homes **smarter**."

He told Eli about his mother's bread, about turning "extra dough" into a tiny, deliberate bread-selling side job from the doorway. About Karim's uncle using his house as a workshop. About Daria's family renting out a small roof room.

"Your home isn't just a roof," he said. "It can be a place that **earns** a little. Or protects what you have. Or grows food. Even if it's just a corner where you run a small trade."

"And one day," he added, "if you can choose, aim to turn rent into ownership, slowly. It's a long goal. But the years will pass anyway."

6. Future You

He tapped the little old man face.

"Sixth," he said. "Don't forget **Future Eli**."

Eli rolled his eyes. "I'm trying not to forget Present Eli."

"Exactly why Future Eli needs your help," Nadan said. "You will not always be young and strong. A cart can break your leg. A sickness can slow you. Time will definitely slow you."

He drew a small pouch and marked it with a symbol.

"From everything you earn," he said, "take **a small part**—maybe one coin in twenty—and say, 'This is not for now. Not even for this year. This is for old me. For big trouble. For the day I can't run messages anymore.'"

"And never touch it?" Eli asked.

"Touch it when **life** hits," Nadan said. "Not when boredom hits. Not for sweets. Not for showing off. For real storms: sickness, family emergencies, old age."

He shrugged.

"Old Nadan is very grateful to Young Nadan," he said. "And

I'm not even that old yet."

7. Levelling Up

He tapped the hammer again.

"Last one," he said. "You want more money? Don't start with 'How can I get more coins?' Start with:

How can I become more useful?"

Eli frowned. "I just run messages."

"For now," Nadan said. "Could you learn the routes better and be faster than everyone else? Learn to read and write so you can carry important letters, not just spoken words? Learn prices, so merchants trust you with buying and selling?"

Eli thought.

"Maybe," he said. "If someone taught me."

"There are people who will," Nadan said. "A scribe who needs help. A merchant who needs a smart runner. But they like teaching people who **stick around**, not those who vanish after a week."

He leaned back against the tree.

"Every extra skill you add," he said, "is like opening another gate that coins can walk through. Saving and investing matter. But if you also grow your **earning power**, everything multiplies."

Eli stared at the drawings in the dirt.

"So that's it?" he said. "Seven things and I'm fixed?"

"No," Nadan said. "Seven things and you have a direction."

He wiped his hands.

"You'll still mess up," he said. "We did. We still do. There were days I spent stupidly, deals we misjudged, times we almost blew everything. But we had these rules to come back to."

Eli hesitated.

"Who's 'we'?" he asked.

Nadan smiled.

"People who started right here," he said, tapping the dirt. "Four kids who called themselves the Empty Pockets Club."

Eli snorted. "That's a terrible name."

"We upgraded," Nadan said. "To the **First Coins**. Then to the **Builders Club**."

He stood up, brushing off his tunic.

"Come back here tomorrow," he said. "If you're serious, bring whatever you earn today. Even if it's just one coin."

Eli squinted at him. "Why?"

"Because," Nadan said, "you don't learn this stuff by listening. You learn it by **doing**. We'll plan what to do with your **next** coin, not your imaginary millions."

He started to walk away, then paused.

"Oh," he added, "and bring anyone else who's tired of feeling like money is this weird monster that controls their whole life."

He nodded toward the city.

"There's plenty of room under this tree."

Later that afternoon, three familiar figures arrived under the palm.

Bela, now a full trader with two stalls, tossed Nadan a dried fig.

"You recruiting again?" he asked. "Saw you gesturing at the ground like a mad prophet."

"Just talking to myself," Nadan said.

"Liar," Daria said, joining them with a tablet under her arm. "I saw the boy. Smart eyes. Familiar gleam in them."

Karim came last, smelling faintly of sawdust.

"There's a rumour," he said, "that some kid is saying, 'There's this weird group that sits under a tree and talks about coins and the future.'"

"Ah, we're legends now," Bela said. "Terrifying."

They sat down together, as they had a thousand times.

"So," Daria asked, "what did you tell him?"

"The simple version," Nadan said. "Save. Spend wisely. Invest. Protect. Use your home. Plan for future you. Grow skills."

Karim smiled.

"Same old story," he said.

"Same old story," Nadan agreed. "Still works."

The four of them sat in the cooling air, the city moving around them.

They weren't the richest in Babylon.

There were merchants with palaces, landlords with ten houses, traders with ships they'd never seen with their own eyes.

But:

- None of them panicked when work slowed.
- Their homes were stronger, their families less fragile.
- They had savings, investments, and skills that could rebuild even if disaster hit.
- They could help others sometimes, Rafi, Mina, that cart driver, people like Eli—without collapsing themselves.

They were not invincible.

They were **prepared**.

Bela stretched, looking at the carving of their old name on the palm trunk.

"Do you ever miss being the Empty Pockets Club?" he asked.

"No," they all said at once.

They laughed.

Daria tapped her stylus against her tablet.

"Think we'll still be meeting here in twenty years?" she asked.

"If the tree's still standing," Karim said.

"If Babylon's still standing," Bela added.

"If we are," Nadan said. "And even if we're not, maybe someone else will."

He thought of Eli, pacing in the dirt, overwhelmed and frustrated.

People like him would keep being born.
   Money would keep being confusing.
   Bad deals would keep being offered.
   Rent would keep being due.

But there would also be:

- A palm tree.
- A set of simple rules.
- Someone willing to say, "I was as lost as you. Here's what helped."

Maybe that was the real treasure.

Not the coins they'd collected.

The **path** they could pass on.

That evening, as the sun dipped and the city glowed, Eli counted the fresh coins in his hand.

Not many.

But this time, before they could evaporate, he did something new:

He took one coin out of ten and set it aside.

"For Future Me," he whispered.

It felt small.

It felt weird.

It felt… powerful.

Then he looked toward the palm tree and smiled.

"Next," he said quietly to himself.

And for the first time, "next" didn't mean "next disaster."

It meant **next step**.

13

Real World Examples

This chapter shows you **how money works in the real world**, using clear examples, real numbers, and simple explanations anyone can understand.

Nothing here is complicated. Nothing requires advanced maths. These are the same ideas adults struggle with, but when you learn them young, everything becomes easier:

1. Real-Life Budgeting
2. Pay Yourself First & Compound Investing
3. Investing in the S&P 500
4. Buying a Home (Mortgages)
5. Scams & Schemes
6. Bringing It All Together

Section 1: Real-Life Budgeting

Based on a UK Average Starting Salary

Before you can invest, you need to understand **what to do with your first real salary**. Most teens assume you only start budgeting when you're older. The truth: your very first job is the moment you build habits that set you up for life.

A typical first full-time job in the UK pays around **£22,000-£24,000** per year. Let's use **£23,000** as a real example.

Your Real Take-Home Pay

After tax and basic deductions:

- **~£1,650 per month** is what actually lands in your bank. (use an online salary calculator to estimate taxes)

This is the number that matters.

How to Use Your First £1,650 the Smart Way

This simple plan gives you savings, investing, fun, and freedom - all at once.

1. Pay Yourself First - 10%

This is the rule that changes your financial future.

- 10% of £1,650 = **£165/month**
- This goes **straight into your investing account** (S&P 500 fund)
- Set it to automatic so you don't rely on motivation

2. Essentials - around 50%

Example breakdown:

- Shared accommodation: **£550**
- Food: **£150**
- Transport: **£60**
- Phone: **£15**
- Extras: **£100**
- **Total: ~£875**

3. Lifestyle / Fun / Goals - 30%

Money you can use without guilt:

- Clothes
- Gym
- Eating out
- Holidays
- Saving for a car
- Hobbies

Example: **£495 per month**

4. Cushion / Leftover

Depending on your exact costs, you'll have around **£115** left.
This gives you breathing room for emergencies or extra savings.

Why This Works

- You save and invest automatically.
- You cover all essentials.
- You still enjoy life.
- You avoid debt.
- You build habits most adults never learn.

This is the foundation.
Once you master this, the rest of the chapter - investing, compounding, mortgages, and more - becomes easy.

Section 2: Pay Yourself First & Compound Investing

Most people think wealth starts when you "finally earn more." In reality, it starts the moment you decide to **pay yourself first**.

This one habit - taking a small slice of every paycheck and investing it immediately - is the difference between always catching up and getting ahead early.

What Paying Yourself First Looks Like

When money comes in, you do this:

1. **Take your cut first** (your "future money").
2. Put it into your investing account.
3. Live on what's left.

If you're earning £1,650/month in your first job, 10% = **£165/month invested**. If you're still 15–18, it can be £20, £30, £50 - the habit matters.

Why Starting Young Gives You an Unfair Advantage

Ages **15–25** are the easiest years in your entire life to save because:

- You usually have **low expenses**.
- You have **no kids, no mortgage, no major bills**.
- You have **time** - the most powerful part of investing.

Even tiny amounts grow into something meaningful.

Lets look at some simple examples £50 / £150 / £250 per Month (Starting at Age 18)

Using an 8% average yearly return.

£50/month

Age	Value
25	~£7,000
30	~£11,000
35	~£19,000
40	~£30,000
50	~£67,000
60	~£137,000

£150/month

Age	Value
25	~£21,000
30	~£33,000
35	~£57,000
40	~£95,000
50	~£200,000
60	~£410,000

£250/month

Age	Value
25	~£35,000
30	~£55,000
35	~£95,000
40	~£155,000
50	~£330,000
60	~£680,000

Key Lessons

- You don't need to be rich to start investing and to retire with significant savings.
- You just need to start early and be consistent.
- Small amounts invested regularly compound into huge sums over time.
- This sets you up for the S&P 500 section next.

A. Starting Now (Age 15–18)

Most teens think small money doesn't matter. But small money + time = *real results*.

Let's look at **£30/month**.

Example 1: You invest £30/month from age 15 to 18, then STOP

You invest for 3 years only.
Total you put in:
£30 × 12 × 3 = **£1,080**
If that £1,080 grows at a normal long-term average of **8% per year**, here's what it becomes *with no extra money added*:

Age	Approx Value
18	£1,080
25	~£1,850
30	~£2,720
40	~£5,870
50	~£12,700
60	~£27,400

Example 2: You keep investing £30/month from 15 all the way to 60

£30/month = **£360 per year**.
Using the same 8% growth:

Age	Total Invested	Approx Value
18	£1,080	~£1,170
25	£3,600	~£5,200
30	£5,400	~£9,800
40	£9,000	~£26,300
50	£12,600	~£62,000
60	£16,200	~£139,000

Why These Two Examples Matter

- Small amounts grow more than you expect.
- The earlier you begin, the stronger the final numbers.
- The habit is more important than the amount.
- When you move to a better job and invest more (£150–£250/month), the numbers grow even faster.

B. Versus Starting at 30

Now let's compare this to someone who **waits until age 30** to start investing.

They begin at 30 and invest the **same £30/month (£360/year)** until age 60.

If you start at 30 with £30/month

£360/year for 30 years.

Age	Total Invested	Approx Value
30	£0	£0
40	£3,600	~£5,200
50	£7,200	~£11,200
60	£10,800	~£23,000

The Difference Is Massive

By age 60:

- **Starting at 15:** ~£139,000
- **Starting at 30:** ~£23,000

That's a difference of **£116,000** - created entirely by starting early.

Same person. Same job. Same life.

Only difference: **starting early vs. starting late**.

Section 3: Investing in the S&P 500

You might be asking yourself, thats all well and good, but how do i secure a consistent reasonable return on my investment without taking big risks. The answer is simple.

The S&P 500 is one of the easiest and safest ways for beginners to start investing. It's simply a basket of 500 of the biggest companies in America - brands you already know. (You could also choose a UK index like the FTSE 100)

Instead of choosing one company, you buy a tiny piece of all 500 at once.

Why It's Good for Beginners

- You don't need to pick stocks.
- You spread your money across many companies.
- Over long periods, it has historically grown.

We have used a simple example return of 8% per year to keep calculations realistic. (although the S&P has actually averaged 11.8% for the last 20 years)

A word of warning, in investing as in life, past performance is not a guarantee of future success. There will inevitably be, and there have been years where the S&P has performed very poorly, there are also years of massive growth. Both of these are to be ignored when you are playing the long game. The key is slow and steady growth over years. One bad year or one good year dont move the needle that much when you are looking at a 10, 20 or even 40 year investment window. And that is the mindset of the wealthy. Focus on tomorrow not on today. Future you will thank you.

The Key Idea You Must Remember

It's not about picking the perfect stock. It's not about timing the market. It's not about having a huge salary.

It's about:

- Starting early
- Investing every month
- Letting time grow your money

This prepares you for Section 4: **Buying a Home (Mortgages)** - because investing and saving are exactly how you build your deposit.

Section 4: Buying a Home (Mortgages)

The Deposit: Your First Big Goal

In the UK, most first-time buyers need a deposit of around **£50,000–£60,000**.

It sounds huge, but the key is to build slowly over the years.

Here are realistic saving examples over **10 years**:

- **£150/month** → £1,800/year → **£18,000 in 10 years**
- **£200/month** → £2,400/year → **£24,000 in 10 years**
- **£250/month** → £3,000/year → **£30,000 in 10 years**

This is from saving alone. When you are investing, the deposit can build faster.

Real Example: Reaching a £50,000 Deposit in 12 Years

Let's say you start at **age 18** and want a deposit by **age 30**.
   You save and invest **£200/month** at an average growth of 8%.

Your Contributions:

£200/month = £2,400/year.

Over 12 years: **£28,800 saved and invested**.

What It Grows Into (at 8%):

Age	Years Saving	Total Saved	Approx Value
20	2	£4,800	~£5,300
25	7	£16,800	~£22,000
28	10	£24,000	~£36,000
30	12	£28,800	~£46,000

With simple, steady habits, you realistically reach a **£50k deposit by age 30**.

If you keep to the 10% rule, even if you start smaller with £165 per month and increase as your salary increases you can realistically reach your goal.

2. A Real Example: Buying a £300,000 Home

If a home costs **£300,000**, and you have a **£50,000 deposit**, then you borrow:

£300,000 − £50,000 = £250,000 mortgage.

On a standard 25-year mortgage:

- Monthly payments may be roughly **£1,300–£1,500**, depending on interest rates.

Why this matters:

A **bigger deposit** means:

- Smaller monthly payments
- Less stress
- Less total interest paid during the 25 years

3. How Mortgage Interest Works

Interest can be your friend when you're investing - but it's your enemy when you borrow.

If you borrow £250,000 over 25 years, you may repay **£350,000+ in total** once interest is included.

This is why saving a bigger deposit is so powerful:

- You borrow less
- You pay less interest
- You finish paying sooner

4. Why Your Early 20s Matter

If you start adult life with these habits:

- Saving automatically
- Investing monthly
- Budgeting properly

Then by your mid-to-late 20s you can realistically have:

- **£30-50k saved**
- Extra investing growth
- A clear path to a deposit

Most people only start thinking about buying a home at 28–30.

You'll already be ahead.

5. The Real Message

Buying a home is not about:

- Being rich
- Having a great job
- Getting lucky

It's about:

- Consistent saving
- Investing early
- Avoiding bad debt
- Understanding how mortgages work

With good habits and time, buying a home becomes **possible**, not overwhelming.

Section 5: Avoiding Schemes & Scams

1. If someone promises quick money, it's likely a scam

Scammers know people want money fast.
Typical lies you'll hear:

- "Send me £200 and I'll turn it into £600."

- "Guaranteed profit."
- "I'll trade for you."
- "You can't lose."

Real investing takes time. Scams rely on excitement.
If it sounds fast or guaranteed, walk away.

2. Don't invest in anything you don't understand

If you can't explain it in one sentence, don't touch it.
This protects you from:

- Day trading (buying and selling all day trying to time every tiny move)
- Forex and "signals" groups
- Options trading you don't fully understand
- Crypto schemes
- Trading groups
- "Secret strategies"
- Business "Opportunities" with no clear purpose, path or goal

If you're not sure *how* it makes money, you are not investing - you are guessing.
Understanding comes first. Money comes later.

3. Investing is not gambling and gambling is not investing

Gambling is when you risk money on something you **cannot control** and **don't understand**, just hoping to get lucky.

Examples:

- Casinos
- Slots
- Sports betting
- Treating trading apps like a game

It can feel exciting, but the odds are against you. Over time, the house always wins.

Real investing is the opposite:

- You understand what you own
- You spread your risk
- You think in years, not minutes
- You don't rely on luck

If it feels like gambling, it probably is.

4. Never send money to a stranger online

Scammers use:

- Instagram
- TikTok
- Telegram

- WhatsApp
- Fake support chats

They pretend to be:

- Traders
- Mentors
- Influencers
- "Experts"

If someone messages you first - they usually want your money. Don't give it to them, no matter what they promise you.

4. If it feels rushed, pressured, or secret - it's probably fake

Scams use pressure because pressure stops you thinking.
  Red flags:

- "Offer ends today."
- "Keep this quiet."
- "You must act now."

Real opportunities give you time to think.
  Scams try to stop you thinking.

5. Use real platforms only

Safe places for money:

- Your bank's app

- Actual investment platforms
- Reputable crypto exchanges

Danger zones:

- DMs
- Random websites
- Screenshots
- Telegram groups
- Instagram promotions

If someone sends you a link - don't trust it.

6. Don't trust screenshots, photos, or "success stories"

Scammers make themselves *look* rich:

- Fake profits
- Rented cars
- Borrowed houses
- Edited screenshots

They look successful so you drop your guard.
Nothing online proves anything.

7. Build knowledge so you can spot lies instantly

The more you learn:

- Budgeting
- Saving

- Index investing
- Compounding

...the easier it becomes to see scams for what they are.

Knowledge protects you more than anything else.

The Big Message

Scams try to distract you with excitement.
    Real wealth comes from patience.

If you follow these rules:

- You avoid the traps
- You keep your money safe
- You stay on track
- You build a future without losing years of work

Smart beats fast.
    Every time.

Section 6: Avoiding Debt and Escaping It When You're In It

1. Understand What Debt Really Is

Debt is not free money.
Debt is money you borrow from your **future self**.
Future you has to:

- Work more
- Stress more
- Pay interest
- Have fewer choices

Some debt helps you grow (like a mortgage or education).
Most debt holds you back.

2. Avoid High-Interest Debt at All Costs

The worst traps are:

- Credit cards
- Buy Now Pay Later
- Store cards
- Payday loans

They look harmless.
They look small.
They look easy.
But the interest grows faster than your salary.
If you borrow £500 on a card and only pay the minimum,

you can have paid more than that and still be paying it back **years** later.

The rule is simple:

If you can't afford it now, don't buy it now.

3. Don't Borrow for Lifestyle

Never go into debt for:

- Clothes
- Nights out
- Holidays
- Gadgets
- Upgrades
- Trends

Debt for lifestyle is trading long-term peace for short-term excitement.

4. The Only Good Reasons to Use Debt

Use debt only for things that **grow your life**, not drain it.
Good debt:

- A home (stable, long-term value)
- Education (increases earning ability)
- A business (creates income)

Bad debt:

- Anything that loses value the moment you buy it.

If it doesn't make you better, richer, or safer — avoid it.

5. If You Already Have Debt - Here's the Plan

The worst thing you can do is ignore debt.
  It grows in the dark.
  Here's the simple plan to take control:

Step 1: List every debt you have

Write down:

- How much you owe
- The interest rate
- The minimum payment

Step 2: Contact Your Lenders

This is the step most people don't know - but it can save you **months or even years**.
  Call or email your lender and explain:

- You're committed to paying off the debt
- You're building a repayment plan
- You want the debt to stop growing

Ask them directly: **"Can you freeze the interest while I'm paying this down?"**

Many lenders will:

- Freeze interest for a period of time
- Lower the interest rate
- Offer a payment plan you can afford
- In some cases, even reduce part of the debt

Lenders prefer you to repay slowly rather than not at all - so they're often willing to help.

This single conversation can stop the debt from growing and makes your repayment plan much faster

Step 3: Pay the minimum on all, then attack the highest interest one

This is called the **debt avalanche**.
Why it works:

- High-interest debt grows the fastest
- Paying it down first saves the most money

Step 4: Stop using cards while paying them off

No more adding to the balance.
Every pound you stop borrowing is a pound you don't have to repay with interest.

Step 5: Use any extra income to speed it up

Even small boosts help:

- £20 extra per week
- £50 from a side job
- Selling unused things

Small amounts make a big difference when the goal is reducing interest.

6. Build a Small Buffer to Stay Out of Debt

Most people fall into debt because of surprises.
A phone breaks.
A car needs repairs.
A bill comes in.

Start with 5% - 10% of your monthly income as a buffer, try to build up at least 3 months of your salary.
This stops emergencies from becoming debt.

7. The Big Message

Avoiding debt keeps your future free.
Escaping debt gives you your life back.
If you:

- Avoid borrowing for lifestyle
- Only use debt for things that grow your life
- Pay off what you owe with a clear plan

- Build a buffer so emergencies don't knock you down

…you stay in control.
Debt traps people for decades.
You're learning how to avoid the trap completely.

Section 7: Levelling Up

Becoming Valuable, Indispensable, and Building Multiple Streams of Income

1. Your Income Grows When You Grow

Money follows value. The more you can do, the more the world will pay you.

Most people stop learning after school. That's the mistake.
The people who earn more keep adding skills.

Start small:

- Learn how to communicate clearly
- Learn basic finance (budgeting, investing, saving)
- Learn technical skills (Excel, design, coding, data entry)
- Learn how to identify and solve problems instead of waiting for instructions

Every new skill gives you more options.

2. Become the Person People Rely On

Being "indispensable" doesn't mean working non-stop.
It means being the one who:

- Shows up
- Delivers on time
- Doesn't make excuses
- Fixes problems
- Thinks ahead
- Makes life easier for others

This alone sets you apart from 90% of people.

When you become reliable:

- You get promoted
- You get trusted with more responsibility
- You get paid more
- People recommend you for opportunities

Reliability is a superpower.

3. Focus on Skills That Are Always in Demand

Some skills are valuable everywhere, in every industry.
Learn even one of these and your earning potential jumps.

Examples:

- Sales

- Communication
- Project management
- Coding
- Graphic design
- Video editing
- Excel and data skills
- Social media management

You don't need to master all of them. One or two is enough to start.

4. Build Multiple Streams of Income

Never rely on a single income stream.

Most adults struggle because they only have one source of income - their job.

If anything goes wrong, everything collapses.

You can build small, simple streams like:

- A part-time skill (design, video editing, tutoring)
- A small business (reselling, services, creative work)
- Renting equipment or tools
- Helping local businesses with social media
- Creating digital products

None of these needs to be huge.

But adding one extra stream makes your entire life safer.

5. Turn Your Time Into Assets

Time = limited.
   Assets = work for you even when you're sleeping.

Examples of assets you can build:

- Investments
- Skills
- Digital products
- Online content

Every asset you build reduces how hard you need to work in the future.

6. Surround Yourself With People Who Aim Higher

Your environment influences your direction.
   If your friends:

- Complain constantly
- Avoid effort
- Waste money
- Mock self-improvement

…it will hold you back.

Spend time with people who:

- Think big
- Learn new things

- Save and invest
- Work toward goals
- Encourage you

Ambition is contagious.

The Big Message

You don't level up by luck. You level up by choice.

If you:

- Learn skills
- Become reliable
- Build extra income streams
- Grow a little each year

…you become valuable, secure, and independent.

Your goal is simple: **Become the kind of person opportunities chase.**

Printed in Dunstable, United Kingdom